LYTTELTON'S
∽ BRITAIN ∽

HUMPHREY LYTTELTON's family boasts a long line of land-owning, political, military, clerical, scholastic and literary forebears – not a musician among them. He always claimed to have most in common with a former Humphrey Lyttelton who was executed for complicity in the Gunpowder Plot. Humph formed his first jazz band in 1948 and it soon became the leading exponent of traditional jazz in Britain. In 1956 his tune 'Bad Penny Blues' became the first jazz record to get into the Top Twenty. In a long and vigorous musical career Humph played with a vast array of musical talent, from Louis Armstrong to Radiohead. In 1971 Humph was invited to chair the pilot series of *I'm Sorry I Haven't A Clue*, a spin-off from the hit radio series *I'm Sorry I'll Read That Again*. Over the fifty series of *Clue* Humph hosted, the programme became one of the most successful comedy series in the history of BBC Radio, winning every award for radio comedy going, selling over 700,000 cassettes and CDs, and mounting two sell-out tours of the UK in 2007 and 2008. Humph died in April 2008, after celebrating forty years as host of Radio 2's *Best of Jazz* and sixty years as a bandleader.

IAIN PATTINSON wrote Humphrey Lyttelton's scripts for *I'm Sorry I Haven't A Clue* for the thick end of fifteen years. He didn't bother with the clever end. Before writing for Humph, Iain supplied the chairman's script for *the News Quiz* and many opening monologues for *Loose Ends*, also on BBC Radio 4. He was plucked from obscurity to write his first series of *Clue* in 1992 and subsequently went on to be plucked from obscurity twice a year thereafter to repeat the process. Since then he has contributed to countless television and radio comedy shows. A list of performers of his scripts now reads like a 'Y to Z' of British comedy. Projects to which he has contributed have amassed four Sony Gold awards, a Bronze Rose of Montreux, a Viewers' and Listeners' award, a TRIC award and a Cycling Proficiency Badge.

LYTTELTON'S BRITAIN

WRITTEN BY

Iain Pattinson

EDITED BY

Jon Naismith

arrow books

This paperback edition published by Arrow 2010

10 9 8 7 6 5

First published in Great Britain in 2008 by Preface Publishing
20 Vauxhall Bridge Road
London SW1V 2SA

An imprint of The Random House Group Limited

www.rbooks.co.uk
www.prefacepublishing.co.uk

Addresses for companies within The Random House Group Limited
can be found at www.randomhouse.co.uk

The Random House Group Limited Reg. No. 954009

A CIP catalogue record for this book is available from the British Library

ISBN 978 1 84809 173 3

The Random House Group Limited supports The Forest Stewardship Council (FSC), the leading international forest certification organisation. All our titles that are printed on Greenpeace-approved FSC-certified paper carry the FSC logo. Our paper procurement policy can be found at www.rbooks.co.uk/environment

Printed and bound in Great Britain by CPI Bookmarque, Croydon CR0 4TD

This book is for Humph

1921–2008

⟡ CONTENTS ⟡

Mr Lyttelton's personal Winnebago, generously funded by the BBC

⫷ INTRODUCTION ⫸

IT WAS 1991. I'd only completed a few months as a trainee producer at the BBC when I was summoned to the office of HLER (that's BBC acronym for Head of Light Entertainment Radio). 'The producer of *I'm Sorry I Haven't A Clue* will be moving on to other things,' said HLER. 'We think you'd make a good replacement'. Up till then I'd barely produced any programmes at all and must have looked a little shaken. 'Don't worry, you'll be fine,' said HLER. 'Just remember to laugh at all their jokes'.

The standard procedure in BBC Radio Entertainment at the time was for new producers to serve an apprenticeship on a show before attempting to operate it themselves. Since the next series of *Clue* wasn't due to start for a couple of weeks, I just sat in my office and awaited instruction. After a week or so had passed, I paid a visit to Janet Staplehurst (the programme's long-serving production assistant) to ask for news of the producer's imminent return from the Edinburgh Fringe. 'His show's going down rather better than expected,' said Janet. 'He's decided to stay up there. You'll have to produce the series yourself.' My mind raced and I felt slightly sick. The ever-efficient Janet was reassuring: 'Don't worry. The studio's booked – and the team.' I felt heartened. 'And who writes the links for Humphrey Lyttelton?' I asked. 'You do,' she replied.

Even less impressive than my track record as a producer then were my credits as a broadcast scriptwriter. Up till 1991 – nothing. Not a scrap. When the day of my first recording as producer of *I'm Sorry I Haven't A Clue* arrived, and I finally introduced myself to its seventy-year-old chairman Humphrey Lyttelton, my face was still aching from an afternoon of sycophantic forced merriment in the company of the rest of the *Clue* team. It was with not a little trepidation that I handed Humph the script for the show. I was expecting at the very least a critical eye to be cast over my efforts, before various jokes were cut out or hastily re-written. Instead, he thanked me politely and didn't give the script a second glance. When the recording started my heart was in my mouth. Then, as the show's opening signature tune faded into audience applause, suddenly and quite palpably, I began to understand the genius of the man. With effortless timing, natural ease and unforced charm he took my fledgling script and made it fly. Not only was he able to elicit gales of laughter where the best I'd hoped for was the occasional flurry, but, most remarkably, he was able to conjure audience hilarity from a simple pause, an inflection, a sigh, a shift of tone, even from silence. It was a complete and towering tour de force and in minutes my mood changed from near hyperventilating panic to the most indescribable joy. That night I was seized with one single-minded determination: to ensure Humphrey Lyttelton's scripts were as good as they could possibly be.

Some months later, during a brief stint producing *The News Quiz*, I found myself working with a writer called Iain Pattinson. Iain was unlike most of the young, faintly unkempt, university-educated writers who filtered their way into the Radio

Entertainment department in the hope of a commission. After a short and unexceptional education in Sidcup, Iain had worked as a market stall holder, insurance broker and marketing executive in the oil industry, before taking early retirement to pursue a dream of writing comedy. Despite his relatively advanced years, a fizzing resentment at the apparent preferment of his Oxbridge-educated peers seemed to lend him a certain youthful vigour. Unlike the department's other writers, Iain was not only 'life educated', he was also financially secure. Quite early in his new career as a writer, he was offered a job on Channel 4's all-new *Clive Anderson Talks Back*, a job offer that any of his colleagues would have jumped at without hesitation. Iain took one look at the fee and declined, with the words: 'That's less than I pay my gardener'. I liked that. And I realised also that the wonderful material he was writing for *The News Quiz* could be done infinitely more justice were it delivered by Humphrey Lyttelton.

So it was that I bequeathed to Iain the role of Humphrey's link writer, in turn heralding the most significant writer/performer relationship in Radio Comedy since Galton & Simpson began writing for Tony Hancock. For sixteen years Iain has written for Humphrey some of the most unfalteringly brilliant and enduring comic lines ever heard on a British wireless, lines which have in turn been delivered with an incomparable skill, style and charm.

Having attempted the job myself, I was well placed to appreciate the difficulty Iain faced, week after week, trying to come up with an amusing introduction to each edition of the programme. Writers on panel shows that draw their material from specific areas such as news, sport or music, immediately have a peg on which to hang their opening material. The problem Iain faced was that *I'm Sorry I Haven't A Clue* draws its inspiration from no single theme. However, we swiftly discovered that by taking the show on the road, not only did we lose our London audience of elderly bag ladies, foreign tourists and assorted oddballs seeking shelter from the cold, but most significantly, we gained a location around which to frame Iain's introductory lines. At first these introductions were no more than a couple of paragraphs, but they soon developed into extended comic histories of the place visited, hugely appreciated by the local theatre audience and one of the most popular elements of the programme as a whole.

Iain's great skill was not only to write wonderfully funny material, it was also his complete understanding of the character of 'Chairman Humph', the unwilling, aristocratic, sometimes irritable, frequently baffled, occasionally louche, often semi-comatose chairman of Britain's most popular radio panel game. Over the years Iain's opening material for *I'm Sorry I Haven't A Clue* has evolved into the almost comprehensive UK gazetteer you have in your hands today. Every page of it seems to resonate with the character and personality of Chairman Humph. It serves as both a reminder of, and tribute to, one of the most brilliant, unique and best-loved broadcasting talents I ever expect to see in my lifetime.

Jon Naismith

ENGLAND
LONDON

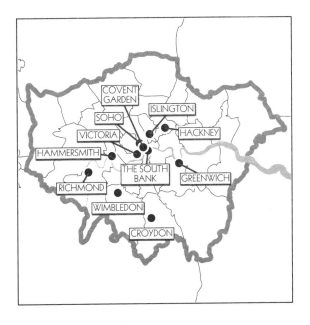

GREENWICH

✠⚜✠

GREENWICH is a London borough which rightly prides itself in a rich history spanning many centuries of Royal association. In 1415, Henry V landed in Greenwich after his return from the Battle of Agincourt, when the vastly superior French horsemen were comprehensively routed by our English archers. But then ten minutes of Linda Snell is enough to terrify anyone.

Henry's military success thus secured France as a market for fine British meat products, and to teach them a lesson, he decreed that export cattle should be fed on diseased sheep carcasses, in the certain knowledge the French would never notice.

Elizabeth I came to Greenwich in 1580 to knight Francis Drake in reward for his round the world voyage. Townsfolk flocked to witness the sight of Good Queen Bess taking up a large sword to perform his circumnavigation ceremony. This was before English spellings were standardised, and as the result of a slight but painful misunderstanding, the words 'Arise, Sir Francis' were entirely wasted on him.

In the 17th Century, architect Christopher Wren did much to set the style of Greenwich when his colonnaded, Neo-Renaissance Royal Naval College was commissioned. However, this was only after his original design, of a huge, upside-down

3

Royal Naval College, Greenwich, 1948.
(The law was later changed, making it illegal to keep women
in large aquariums)

Tupperware bowl held up by string attached to big sticks, was rejected on the grounds the town wanted something visitors might bother to come and see.

Greenwich is also famous for its long associations with literature. Christopher Marlowe frequented local taverns and was supposedly killed in one during a brawl with friends over the bill for dinner. The theory that Marlowe didn't actually die but assumed a new identity as William Shakespeare is supported by the line from *Twelfth Night*: 'If music be the food of love, play on, but there's no way I had a prawn cocktail starter.'

Local residents have included the intellectual and pioneering landscape gardener John Evelyn, who is mentioned by his neighbour Samuel Pepys in the diaries which he wrote in Greenwich in his own special code. As a result, Evelyn has a local pub named after him: 'The Dot, Dot, Dash, Dash, and Bucket'.

The same century saw the founding of the Royal Observatory in Greenwich Park. The finely crafted lenses of its Newtonian telescope gave an unprecedented view of the Northern skies right up until the 1980s, when it had to be moved after someone built a bloody great office block in the way at Canary Wharf.

CROYDON

℘Ⴔ℘

THE SOUTH LONDON suburb of Croydon boasts a rich and varied history. Croydon was first noted as the London residence of the Archbishops of Canterbury, who lived at Addington Palace. When the palace needed to be refurbished in 1807, the Archbishop asked for Capability Brown, but the General Synod decreed he should have Dulux Satin El Paso Beige.

In 1953 Addington Palace became the home of the Royal College of Music, where they pioneered the use of hypnosis for the treatment of those performers who suffered stage fright. At their first concert, the conductor proudly counted his orchestra in, and the entire string section fell into a deep sleep.

Still preserved in the centre of Croydon are its famous Elizabethan Whitgift almshouses. When they were opened in 1599, the mayor proclaimed there was free food and shelter and invited the town's poor, needy and impotent. Well, the poor and the needy arrived, but the impotent couldn't come.

Croydon's ancient parish church was rebuilt by the architect Giles Gilbert-Scott, who famously also designed our traditional red telephone boxes. Sadly Gilbert-Scott died before completion, but as a mark of respect at his funeral, male mourners patiently waited their turn to urinate in his tomb.

In the early 19th Century, Croydon was established as a suburb for middle-class commuters working in the city. And when the East Croydon Railway opened in May 1839, its service reached London Bridge Station in 15 minutes. Just the once.

London's first international aerodrome opened nearby soon after the First World War. However, by the 1950s it was realised that Croydon Airport was too small. A study was undertaken which proved the airport to be hopelessly unable to cope with either London's modern air traffic or passenger numbers, and was therefore judged: 'perfect'.

Long before Charles Darwin's studies, a noted local biologist named Alfred Russell Wallace came up with an early theory of evolution. It was Wallace who coined the phrases 'natural selection' and 'survival of the fittest', to which, when Darwin's book was published, he added 'thieving bastard'.

Other famous names associated with Croydon include that of Matthew Fisher, the former keyboard player with Procul Harem. In a landmark court case in 2007, Fisher was judged to have been co-writer of their record 'A Whiter Shade of Pale', and so immediately sought leave to appeal.

The cricketer Mark Butcher is from Croydon. Having played county cricket for Surrey for several seasons, in 1997 Butcher was selected to play test matches for England. After a few games, he became plagued by injury, his form declined badly and he was promoted to captain.

The international basketball player Luol Deng lives in Croydon. He arrived in South Norwood in 1998 as a young boy with his family, refugees fleeing civil war in Sudan. The family spent an uncertain six months applying for asylum before the Home Office agreed the situation there was so bad, they should be allowed to leave South Norwood.

Croydon's Fairfield Halls found national fame as the home of professional wrestling. When ITV decided to stop broadcasting wrestling, the Fairfield Halls claimed they were badly hurt by the loss of revenue, but they weren't really. More recently the Fairfield Halls appeared briefly in the movie of the *Da Vinci Code*. The halls and surrounding area were used to depict Notre Dame Cathedral and the Isle de la Cité in Paris, making that scene amongst the most convincing in the whole film.

Croydon is noted as home to the first ever self-service Sainsbury's in England. When its doors opened in February 1958, thousands of Croydon's eager residents rushed in to clear the shelves of an unimagined range of goods, thus heralding the golden age of shoplifting.

The winner of 'Weight Watcher of the Year', 1967, leaving Croydon Town Hall

WIMBLEDON

ℵ✿ℬ

WIMBLEDON is a vibrant borough located at the very heart of London's glitzy outskirts. It also has a rich and vibrant history.

The original village first became known in Tudor times, when, in 1587, the Earl of Exeter established the Royal College of Tennis in Wimbledon in an attempt to fulfil Queen Elizabeth I's wish to see an English player compete in a singles final. It is obviously far too soon to say whether his efforts will be rewarded. The Earl himself, however, did go on to achieve his ambition of entering Queens.

Wimbledon village and 400 acres of prime land were under the ownership of the Cecil family until 1638, when King Charles I bought the property as a birthday present for his wife, Henrietta Maria. Sadly, it was not only the wrong size and colour, but it also made her bum look big.

In Regency times, the village became a fashionable haunt for the likes of Lady Hamilton, who scandalised polite society with her many suitors. This held dire consequences for Lord Nelson when he wagered drunkenly at the gaming table: 'If Lady Hamilton isn't completely faithful to me, and me alone, you can pull my arm off and poke me in the eye with it.'

In Victorian times, both Liberty and William Morris produced fabrics in Wimbledon, while Lord Cardigan fought a duel on the common to promote his range of popular knitwear. Subsequently he went on to manufacture the cosy woollen headgear developed during the Crimean War which he named in memory of the Battle of Bobble Hat.

One of the most infamous duels to be fought on Wimbledon Common was in 1803 when the town's MP, Sir Francis Burdett, was challenged by the Duke of York. Burdett was offered the choice of rapier or pistol, and, as an accom-plished swordsman, chose the rapier. It didn't do him much good. The Duke chose the pistol.

May Sutton, the first foreign player to win at Wimbledon

By the 1890s, Wimbledon was well established as a commuter town, with regular horse buses running to the city. However, when the electric tramline arrived in 1907, the horses went to London on that instead.

Wimbledon is probably most famous for its tennis tourna-ment, which began in 1877. Until 1905, players were exclusively English, but then a 14-year-old American girl, May Sutton, was allowed an entry and, at her first attempt, won the Ladies' Singles, the Men's Singles, the Men's Doubles, the Ladies' Doubles, the Mixed Doubles and the Meat Raffle.

During the war, Wimbledon's Centre Court was dug over as

part of the 'dig for victory' campaign, and groundsmen report that vegetables occasionally pop up even to this day. A small turnip which appeared on the baseline in 1998 was blamed for putting Tim Henman out of the quarter finals, when it beat him three sets to love.

In 1985 Boris Becker created a record when he became the first unseeded player to win the men's title. Becker's last match was in 1999, when he was again unseeded, this time by a Russian model in a broom cupboard.

The inventor of the milk carton, Arthur Reynolds, had a small mill in Wimbledon producing cardboard. After devising the new carton, Reynold's business expanded rapidly and he built a large, new factory and warehouse. Sadly, he died at the grand opening, when half the contents spilled out on top of him.

During the 1960s, the French philosopher and dramatist Jean-Paul Sartre came to live and work in Wimbledon. An exponent of atheistic existentialism, it was during his time in the borough that Sartre wrote *Les Chemins de la Liberté* and *Les Wombles de la Commonne de Wimbledon*. He left England shortly after, complaining he'd been plagiarised by a TV series, called *Les Chemins de la Liberté de Noddy et Big Ears*.

Wimbledon was also the birthplace of Samuel Cunard, of shipping line fame. Cunard left school at the age of 12 but could find no work. Finding an abandoned rowing boat on the Thames at Mortlake, he repaired it and began ferrying passengers across for a penny a time. With the cash he bought more old rowing boats and patched them up, until after twenty years of tirelessly repairing and rowing, working sixteen-hour days, seven days a week, Cunard's rich uncle died and left him a shipping line.

RICHMOND

ॐ✿ॐ

RICHMOND is one of London's most outlying boroughs, situated as it is in North Yorkshire. This interesting community was described in 1945 by the British Council Guide as: 'the most typically British town'. Bearing in mind that in 1945 most British towns had typically been reduced to rubble, this is some compliment indeed. Richmond today is a thriving, bustling place mainly concerned as it is with the thriving bustle manufacturing industry.

Just across the River Thames from the town proper, is the site now famous as the place where it was decided Henry VIII would have his magnificent Hampton Court. On hearing this, the Royal Tailor thought to put an extra gusset in Henry's new trousers. Henry took the Palace from Wolsey to provide a home for his new wife Anne Boleyn. However, she was never comfortable there, complaining that the ceilings were too low. Structural alterations were found to be impossible, as the building was Grade II listed by the English Council for the Preservation of Modern Buildings, and so the king took the only alternative, which was to have Anne Boleyn shortened by a foot or so.

HAMMERSMITH

৪ঢ়৪

HAMMERSMITH is the West London borough boasting a certain amount of history. Actually, the very name 'Hammersmith' has an interesting derivation. Local historians have discovered it comes from an early Saxon word 'Hamm-oder-stythe', which literally means 'Hammersmith'. Early in 2008, archaeologists had to be summoned when repair work on the A4 slip road unearthed evidence of a pre-Christian pagan temple of unusual provenance. Believing their rituals would bring them fertility and favour from their pagan gods, ancient Hammersmith peasants in tall, pointed masks waved flaming torches as they danced around naked virgins smeared with the blood of freshly slaughtered swans. Obviously, the archaeologists had to ask them to stop while they looked at the temple.

For many years, the borough of Hammersmith was home to the White City athletics venue. It was completed just in time for London to host the 1908 Olympics, which were originally scheduled to take place in Rome. But just a month before the games were due to start, Mount Vesuvius erupted with an almighty explosion, at which point Italy immediately surrendered.

The Hammersmith Studios were once the home of the satellite channel Live TV, which was responsible for putting Topless Darts on our screens. And in the cause of research for this book,

I was supplied with a DVD of it. I can't possibly describe quite how disgusted I was by the sight of the big wobbly breasts of Jocky Wilson and Eric Bristow.

A question mark hangs over the future of the Hammersmith light bulb factory

Sadly now long gone, the Osram manufacturing plant was at nearby Brook Green. Since the factory closed down, it's been empty for many years while debates rage amongst a succession of redevelopers about how best to convert the building. So we still don't know how many architects it takes to change a light bulb factory.

VICTORIA

⊗🙵⅋

ERHAPS THIS AREA'S most famous attraction is Tate
Britain, the art gallery established on the site of the old
Millbank Prison. During recent renovation work,
evidence of the building's previous use was discovered in the
form of a slopping-out bucket which had lain un-emptied for
over a century. A workman in breathing apparatus dragged the
fetid bucket out into the main hall, where it promptly won that
year's Turner prize. A strange piece of art, maybe, but one
judged by critics to be particularly fine, as the flies follow you
round the room.

The gallery was founded by the philanthropist Henry Tate
who made his millions from selling sugar cubes. A statue of him
erected in front of the gallery recently needed urgent restoration
work, after the teeth fell out.

Attempting to gain wider appeal, the Tate has expanded in
recent years, with Tate Modern, Tate Liverpool, Tate St Ives and
their touring show: Tate That.

The child prodigy Mozart was brought to London by his
parents and lived for a time in Victoria's Ebury Street, where, at
the age of four, he wrote his first two symphonies – in Ah Major
and Guh Minor.

In the early 19th Century, French prisoners of the Napoleonic
War were housed in prison ships moored on the Thames at

nearby Millbank. However, these ships regularly sank until it was discovered prisoners were tunnelling their way out.

Victoria Station, London's second busiest railway terminus after Waterloo, services both the Orient and Gatwick Express. In the financial year 2006/07, Gatwick Airport received just over 23 million passengers. It hopes to get them boarded soon.

Victoria Coach Station, boarding a bus with her husband,
Derek Coach Station and friends

But a stone's throw from Victoria Station is the Victoria Palace Theatre, where an early performer was the world-famous ballerina Pavlova. In 1911, the great French chef Georges Auguste Escoffier created a dessert pudding in her honour, which he delivered to the theatre in person. However, before the dessert could be sampled, the doorbell rang, and Pavlova's dogs ate it. The famous bronze statue of Pavlova in front of the theatre was removed in 1939. The theatre management can't say whether its metal was taken for the war effort to make bombs, or whether it ended up in someone's garden. The answer is: both.

The radio and TV comedian Professor Stanley Unwin made regular appearances at the Victoria Palace. Despite his apparent jolly demeanour, Unwin was in fact a life-long sufferer of clinical depression, admitting to frequent bouts of feeling suicidallo.

The founder of the interior design and furnishings concern, Laura Ashley, lived in Victoria. Once a flourishing business, in the 1990s the company's financial position declined, and although never actually in the red, they were occasionally in the Autumn Russet.

SOHO

༄༙༄

URING the 17th Century, many settlers moved to Soho from mainland Europe. These included Greek crafts-men fleeing Ottoman domination, as they were unable to compete with discount Turkish sofas.

These were followed by successive waves of refugees escaping religious persecution, including Polish Catholics, French Huguenots and German Lutherans. Evidence of this is found in names such as Greek Street and the famous French House pub, but migrant assimilation wasn't without its troubles, particularly when the Germans invaded Poland Street.

Despite its seedy reputation, Soho has been the home of many famous names. These include the eminent physicist John Dalton, who pioneered research into colour blindness when he discov-ered he was unable to distinguish blue light from red. This became apparent when Dalton went into Berwick Street police station, slapped a half-crown on the desk and asked for twenty minutes with Easy Lil from Muswell Hill.

The German philosopher and founder of modern commu-nism, Karl Marx, lived with his family in a small flat in Gerrard Street in horribly overcrowded conditions, until Harpo and Groucho moved out.

Another famous former resident of Soho was author Washington Irving, who in addition to his most famous work *Rip Van Winkle*, also wrote many other medical text-books.

In the art world, Soho was home to the artist Canaletto, and it was while living in Soho that he famously painted *Westminster Bridge at Dusk*. Completed in vivid oils, Westminster Council complained they'd only wanted it brushed over with Hammerite.

Hilaire Belloc, the poet and historian, lived in Gerrard Street, in the heart of Chinatown. He lodged there at number 28, or as the locals call it, 'Special Fried Szechuan Noodles'.

Soho, 1952

In the late sixties, Soho was home to Jimi Hendrix, who overcame his dyslexia to become one of the world's greatest rock guitarists. Sadly, Hendrix died there in 1970, after choking on his own Vimto.

On Soho's outskirts is the famous London Palladium. From the 1860s until the turn of the century, the Palladium building was a successful amusements arcade, but as the century turned, fortunes declined. These were reversed in 1906 with the opening of the innovative Oxford Circus tube station, when crowds flocked to gaze in awe at the sight of a moving escalator. London Underground recently announced plans to celebrate the event by repeating the spectacle.

Britain's greatest pianist, Russ Conway,
spent several years staring at the London Palladium

The Palladium building was frequently refurbished and proudly boasted it was the first theatre in Britain to be entirely carpeted, a luxury made affordable in 1910 as it coincided with the start of Allied Carpets' closing down sale.

With the decline of music hall in the 1920s, the Palladium was refurbished once again and turned to staging great spectaculars, including one show of North American Apache Indians. Sadly, the first night was plunged into darkness, when it was found the theatre had been rewired by a bunch of cowboys.

Early performances at the Palladium included the novelty act George Robey, who appeared as 'Burlington Bertie', the 'Singing Toilet Bowl'.

Judges setting off for the National Baked Bean Eating Championships

As its fortunes progressed, the theatre attracted big names from America, such as Harry Houdini. It is recorded, however, that his audience became restless as Houdini's opening night was delayed by nearly an hour, when he got locked in the lavatory. After his death, Houdini's son inherited his father's secrets and went on to invent the CD case.

Probably the most famous Soho thoroughfare is Carnaby Street. Once known as the centre of 'Swinging London' that title fell into disuse with the abolition of capital punishment.

COVENT GARDEN

☙❦☙

OVENT GARDEN was designed by Inigo Jones after the style of the architecture of Venice. When the refurbished Covent Garden piazza was reopened in 1980, an international football match was screened there in celebration, with the Venetian team winning a thrilling game after extra time. As an enthusiastic commentator noted at the time, there was dancing in the streets of Venice that night.

In Victorian times, Covent Garden became the haunt of ne're-do-wells and prostitutes. Prime Minister Gladstone took to patrolling the area by night and taking fallen women back to his home to teach them the evils of sin, and sure enough, within a few weeks, he'd learnt the joys of it.

On the east side of Covent Garden is Bow Street, home of the famous Bow Street Runners, which from 1749 to 1829 won every year's 'Best String Bean Display'.

With increasing traffic congestion, in 1974 the old Covent Garden fruit and vegetable market closed, and its greengrocers moved to Nine Elms. They actually wanted to move to Eight Elms, but it was a bit over.

In addition to its many shops and bars, Covent Garden is also home to the London Transport Museum, where visitors can enjoy a static display of vintage underground carriages. Alternatively, they can save a few quid by taking a trip on the Northern Line.

*A keen listener joins the queue
for a recording of*
Gardeners' Question Time

At the beginning of World War II, Covent Garden had become the home of many immigrants from central Europe. It is recorded that a young German woman named Helga Schmidt, suspected of being a spy, was hidden in a Covent Garden loft by a local shopkeeper. Completely penniless, Fraulein Schmidt offered him sexual favours in return for food and protection. What a relief it was for Fraulein Schmidt when she learnt the war was over, in 1978.

Long Acre is also home to the headquarters of the National Association of Second-hand Car Dealers, who claim a membership of 25,000, although the true figure is probably more than twice that.

On the south-west corner of Covent Garden is Trafalgar Square, where every December is erected a huge Christmas tree sent by the people of Norway. They also send funds to provide workmen to spend the other eleven months picking needles out of the pigeons.

Just north of Trafalgar Square is the National Portrait Gallery, which has in recent years courted controversy with several avant garde works, including a less than flattering portrait of Richard Branson. The Virgin boss has huge, yellow teeth, great puffy red

*Trafalgar Square Christmas tree with decorations by
the Dutch artist Piet Mondrian*

lips, and leers menacingly through green eyes under hideous
bushy brows, and the picture tries to convey this.

Along the nearby Strand is Coutts Bank, who have for

generations handled the finances of the Royal Family. As a young girl of seven, Queen Elizabeth was visited by the manager of Coutts to discuss a small loan. And after chatting with him, she duly agreed to let them have one.

Nestling between the districts of Covent Garden and Soho can be found the London Coliseum on St Martin's Lane, home of the English National Opera. In the Edwardian era the Coliseum ran horse races on the theatre's famous revolving stage, which operated like a running machine. One evening however, it malfunctioned and suddenly stopped. This explains why the pub next door has four horses' heads on the wall, and above them, the heads of four very surprised little jockeys.

In August 1914, the future Queen Mother was brought to the Coliseum by her parents to celebrate her fourteenth birthday. In the afternoon they took in a matinée, and on the way home war was declared on Germany. She said she'd have been just as happy with a pony.

THE SOUTH BANK

૪૭૪

L ONDON'S SOUTH BANK owes much to the Millennium
celebrations, which really helped the area to develop as
a tourist attraction. Today thousands come to the South
Bank and pay a few pounds to enjoy an uninterrupted 45-minute
viewing of London and the Thames, as they wait for their
Network South-East train to finally crawl off Hungerford
Bridge. Or they can climb up to the top of the mighty tower of
the Shell Centre to enjoy a panoramic vista right across half of
London. You can't see the other half because some fool has put a
seven-hundred foot bicycle-wheel in the way.

Just along the Thames embankment is found County Hall.
Once the home of the Greater London Council, the building is
now a hotel of international repute, providing foreign business-
men somewhere to stay in luxury, while on visits to Britain
closing down car factories.

The area has benefited from the 3.5 billion pound Jubilee
Line extension to the Millennium Dome. Possibly the only
stretch of London underground where each passenger is guaran-
teed an empty coach.

The South Bank is perhaps most famously known as the home
of the National Theatre. A national theatre for Britain was originally proposed by the publisher Effingham Wilson in 1848. The
project was completed in record time for a public building, and

was in use as early as 1976. During much of his dealings with the builders, Effingham Wilson was in fact Effingham Daily.

The National Theatre is of controversial post-modern design, once described by Prince Charles as a 'monstrous carbuncle on the face of a much-loved friend', until an aide pointed out that he was actually looking at the National Gallery.

The National actually comprises three stage venues: The Olivier, which is named after Sir Laurence Olivier, the Cottesloe, which isn't named after Sir Laurence Olivier, and the Lyttelton, named after a relative of mine, Oliver Lyttelton, 1st Viscount Chandos, and the theatre's first chairman. Oliver, or, as I knew him, 'Uncle Viscount Chandos', joined the government in 1940 when a House of Commons seat was found for him at Aldershot. Which explains why he had to shout during Prime Minister's Questions. In his capacity as Head of Non-Ferrous Metals, Oliver organised the war-effort campaign to collect pots, pans and kettles for the RAF. But Bomber Command found that dropping high explosives was more effective.

Since Oliver's time as chairman, the National has seen many varied productions, from Beckett's *Happy Days*, famously featuring Dame Peggy Ashcroft in the lead role of 'the Fonz', through to Michael Bogdanov's controversial 1980 staging of *The Romans in Britain*. The graphic scenes of Roman soldiers ravishing young British men prompted Mary Whitehouse to bring a private prosecution for obscenity. The result of her detailed evidence of the physical act was the banning from the London stage of any scene depicting explicit leapfrog.

ISLINGTON

⸘⸕⸘

SETTLEMENT in Islington was first mentioned in Anglo-Saxon times as Gislandune, or 'Hill of Gisla'. No one now knows who Gisla was and in modern times the name is only ever used by the drug-crazed sadist who sets the Daily Telegraph Cryptic Crossword. The hill is recorded as being close to the site where Boadicea (originally pronounced 'Boodikka' before later being pronounced dead) fought the Romans at Islington Spa, before taking on the Iceni at Camden Sainsburys.

Fleeing from London in 1372, Edward II was captured close by Islington in what was then Middlesex forest. The hapless monarch later suffered a painful death at the hands of a torturer wielding a red hot poker after uttering those famous last words: 'You know where you can stick that for a start'.

Later still, Sir Walter Raleigh settled briefly in Islington. The man who had successfully introduced the nation to potatoes and tobacco set about opening his famous bicycle factory in Upper Street. It soon became fashionable at court to be seen riding either the Raleigh Tourer or the Raleigh BMX and it is widely rumoured that Queen Elizabeth I herself spent many happy afternoons astride the sturdy Raleigh Chopper.

Today, Islington is the haunt of artists and writers, a trend started by Daniel Defoe. Working on early drafts of *Robinson*

Crusoe he found himself wanting for a character name. Glancing round his study, Defoe's eye fell upon the calendar and a particular day inspired him to name Crusoe's native sidekick: 'Man Pancake'.

Islington has been the home of many famous celebrities, including Tony Blair before he moved to Downing Street. It was at a restaurant in Upper Street that he and Gordon Brown met to debate which of them would become Prime Minister first. Brown lost, and had to accept the job of Chancellor. And then, after tossing the penny again to go double or quits, had to pay for lunch as well. However, he refused to pay the 15 per cent service charge, on the grounds it had to be earned from modernisation of restrictive practices.

Islington began to show evidence of social divide after parts of the borough became fashionable under New Labour

HACKNEY

ℵ✞ℬ

HACKNEY is an ancient community steeped in history. The name 'Hackney' actually derives from a 14th Century French word meaning a workhorse, hence the expression 'Hackney Carriage'. Interestingly the words 'Hackney Carriage' have no connection with Hackney the London borough, which explains why it is impossible ever to find a taxi there.

Hackney is undoubtedly best known for the Hackney Empire. Lasting from about 750 AD well into the 12th Century, it covered much of Northern Europe to the Urals, and was the constant rival to the expansionist Visigoths, who feared the frequent raids into their territory made by fierce marauding warriors clad in sequined suits and large floppy hats, who terrified the indigenous population with plates of jellied eels. Though today the only reminder of the great Hackney Empire is a Grade II listed Victorian theatre on Mare Street, the habit of frightening foreigners with jellied eels and funny hats still remains.

Down the years, the Hackney Empire theatre has seen performances from music hall greats such as Charlie Chaplin, W. C. Fields, Marie Lloyd and Mary Pickford. After one memorable evening when all four appeared on the bill together, Chaplin and W. C. Fields decided to form a business partnership and United Artists was born. Miffed at having been left out, Marie Lloyd started a high street bank to provide finance for Mary Pickford to launch her world famous removals firm.

ENGLAND
THE SOUTH-EAST

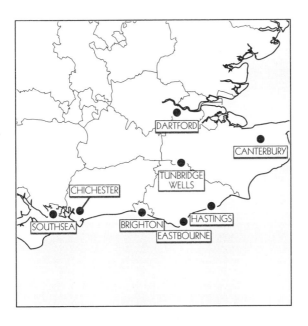

*Network South East put the final touches to the Kent section
of the Eurostar rail link*

DARTFORD

჻ ♔ ჻

THE HISTORIC TOWN of Dartford has much to fascinate the curious visitor. Dartford has been occupied by man since the dawn of civilisation, and at various times animal species as diverse as cave lions, rhinos, tree monkeys and bison roamed the area, until someone thought to fit a new padlock on the zoo gates.

In prehistoric times, the area was the habitat of a vast number of lemmings. As the Ice Age receded, cave paintings record their migration north across the still frozen River Thames to Essex, where, after a short stay, they took up the habit of throwing themselves off cliffs.

Dartford town really only became established with the arrival of the Romans, who record the village of 'Tarrentford' as home of the Tarrent people – a blond-haired tribe of over-rated irritating gits.

Dartford was but a small village until the Middle Ages, when the town enjoyed rapid growth thanks to the many pilgrims passing through on their way to Canterbury. They would assemble in London under the Charing Cross and pray for a safe day's journey. The tradition of praying at Charing Cross to get to Dartford on the same day survives even now.

The nearby housing estate at Thamesmead was used for location shots in the Stanley Kubrick movie *A Clockwork Orange*.

With its distopian scenes of gratuitous sex and violence and with an invented infantile language, it was a difficult place to film, but Kubrick persevered.

The Peasants Revolt of 1381 started in Dartford, when a poll tax collector's brains were beaten out with a hammer by Wat Tyler, to promote his new roofing trade magazine.

Under the reign of Henry VIII, when the Church of England split from Rome, the pilgrim trade went into decline, and Dartford faced economic collapse. However, to encourage a revival, Henry built a small palace in Dartford, which he used as a retreat while attempting to overcome his addiction to wedding cake.

In 1660, Dartford was struck by the plague. When the epidemic ended, the town's mayor decreed that the mighty bells of Holy Trinity Church be rung constantly for a week. The same week in fact that the tinnitus epidemic started.

A worker at the Frank Dobson Candle Factory, Dartford

During the Industrial Age, Dartford took to making fine wax candles and became the largest producer in Europe. However, with the coming of town gas, demand for candles collapsed and traders found they had wax coming out of their ears.

Fine metalworking soon took over as a principal industry, and until very recently parts were supplied to the luxury car market. At a specialist metal fabrications factory it took one man nearly a year to hand-finish a single radiator grill. So they sacked him.

During World War II, Dartford was the most heavily bombed town in England with large areas being flattened. But when peace resumed, negotiations with the Germans agreed compensation was to be paid for the excellent job they'd done.

The next event of historical interest occurred in 1956, when Dartford's famous tunnel was completed. It was opened by Her Majesty the Queen, to the applause of motorists queuing to be the first through. When she returned to open the new Dartford Bridge some 40 years later, Her Majesty was surprised to recognise the same ones again. Sadly, the opening of the magnificent bridge, which soars high above the Thames, had to be postponed because of the terrible wind that afternoon, so fierce it threatened high-sided vehicles. Her Majesty apologised to the crowd, putting it down to the tin of beans she had for lunch.

Probably the most famous name associated with Dartford is Mick Jagger. His contribution to Dartford is recognised in the town's music and arts venue, 'The Mick Jagger Centre', where elderly men with bad haircuts can take their pick from a selection of 19-year-old bikini-clad Brazilian models.

The unveilling of a 1:100 scale model of the proposed Elizabeth Taylor memorial at Dartford

CANTERBURY

ℵⅅℬ

C ANTERBURY is an historic cathedral city and weekend residence of the Archbishop, who at other times lives at Lambeth Palace. Archbishops have for centuries made annual pilgrimages on foot all the way from South London to Canterbury, all the while singing 'Onward Christian Soldiers', 'Jerusalem' and of course, the piece written specially for the journey 'Doing the Lambeth Walk, Oi!'.

Canterbury has been the inspiration for many works of literature. The best known must be the tales of Chaucer's pilgrims, but of course T. S. Elliot was also stirred by the tragic story of the death of Thomas à Becket to write his *Old Possum's Book of Practical Cathedral Murders*.

Historians have recently established that 'Thomas à Becket' was actually simply called 'Thomas Becket' and that his nightclub on West Street was in fact simply called the 'Whisky Go Go'.

With its Marlowe Theatre and Marlowe Exhibition, Canterbury will always also be connected with the mysterious Marlowe, though quite why Raymond Chandler should have based his LA gum shoe private detective stories in South East England is even more of a mystery.

Canterbury is set deep in the Kentish rolling green countryside, for centuries referred to as the 'Garden of England'.

However, with the new direct rail link to Brussels from nearby Ashford, Kent has become known as the 'Patio of Belgium'.

The carving of the Eurostar link through the county's rich agricultural land was the cause of much controversy at the time, but now with the benefit of hindsight, we are beginning to see the undoubted benefits of rail links with the continent. Parisians can now hail a taxi in the Champs-Elysées or the Rue Montmartre to the Gard du Nord at 11am, speed their way effortlessly at 130 mph through the tunnel before noon, and by two o'clock be stuck at a points failure just outside Orpington.

TUNBRIDGE WELLS

☒✿☒

ROYAL TUNBRIDGE WELLS is a splendid Regency town in the county of Kent. Although Kent was the first part of England to be colonised by the Romans, they never settled in Tunbridge Wells, having been frightened off by the local tribes' fearsome house prices.

The area suffered a decline in the 16th Century, when a weak and vulnerable populace was cruelly exploited at the hands of a number of landed families. There were the Knatchbulls of Mersham and the Sackvilles of Knole, but things worsened still with the arrival of the notorious Allders of Croydon.

Tunbridge Wells proper was founded in 1606 when natural springs were discovered nearby and the town's mattress industry began.

During the 17th Century, the town began to welcome the well-heeled, due to the absence of shoe-repair shops. Many arrived to take the restorative mineral waters, and even King Charles I came to Tunbridge Wells hoping to cure his chronic dandruff, a problem that was eventually solved by major surgery. Shortly after, Royal Appointment was awarded to his regular brand of shampoo, which was specially renamed 'And Shoulders'.

The elegance of the spa years lives on in the area known as 'The Pantiles', a colonnaded walkway named after the pavement of clay tiles. After her son slipped and fell there, Queen Anne famously paid for Tunbridge Wells to be provided with stone flags, but since no one could get them up the poles, they ended up on the floor.

1735 saw the arrival in Tunbridge Wells of 'Beau' Nash, who appointed himself Master of Ceremonies and formulated some strict rules of etiquette. These included knowing which fork you picked your nose with, and dictated that a gentleman should always take his hat off if a lady walked past the window he was urinating out of.

Rural Kent today is at the forefront of the support of countryside pursuits, a tradition that stretches back to the memorable occasion when the Archbishop of Canterbury was invited by the Reverend Dr Spooner to join the Kentish Hunt.

Small schoolchildren prepare to run, following the ban on fox hunting, 2007

A few miles to the south east, tourists may care to visit Romney Marsh, and discuss the many successful seasons he spent at QPR.

For centuries the main industry around Tunbridge Wells was the production of hops. As a consequence, the countryside is scattered with many oast houses, where Kent's traditional rural crafts are still practised, such as tarting them up and flogging them off for three quarters of a million quid.

On the outskirts of Tunbridge Wells are the interesting sandstone formations known as 'Toad Rock' and 'High Rocks', which are used to train mountaineers. A young Ranulph Fiennes came to Tunbridge Wells to practise and went on to make his first attempt on Annapurna, while her husband was working nights.

Other famous names associated with Tunbridge Wells include William 'Makepeace' Thackeray and Oswald 'Let's Start a War' Mosley. It was while living in the town that Thackeray wrote and published *Vanity Fair*, and then, later, *Woman's Own* and *Motorcycle Monthly*.

BRIGHTON

ᚹᚻᚹ

BRIGHTON is a city boasting a rich culture and history. A settlement is first recorded in Brighton as long ago as 3000 BC, when Celtic Druids practised their ancient worship of oaks, mistletoe and virgins, and indeed oaks and mistletoe are still plentiful in Brighton.

Another ancient settlement was recorded nearby by the Romans, who noted the area for its Neolithic Camp, a style later replaced by the Anglo-Saxon Mince.

In Saxon times, the village developed into a small port, known as 'Bright Thelmstone'; 'Bright' being the Saxon word for 'Shiny' and 'Thelmstone' meaning 'Thelmstone'.

Brighton is now a bustling resort, but the numbers visiting only really started to grow in the 1760s, when Doctor Richard Russell claimed that drinking Brighton's seawater would cure ailments such as asthma, rickets and impotence. This came as good news to the Prime Minister William Pitt, or as he was affectionately known, 'Wheezy, Bandy, Floppy Willy'.

The town boomed thanks to fishing, and Brighton became famous for its sardines and pilchards. It is recorded that when King Ethelred visited in 975, he was presented with the key to the city, which promptly broke off in his hand.

Brighton first became famous during the English Civil War. With his father executed, Prince Charles fled to Brighton, awaiting a ship to France. Seeking an inn to take refuge, he was offered the King's Head. Later, regulations were imposed on street souvenir vendors to prevent them selling body parts.

Much of the southern town had to be reconstructed following the disastrous sea floods of 1705, and this is commemorated in place names such as 'High Tide Alley', 'Basking Shark Blocking the Chimney Street' and 'Where's my Snorkle? (I Need to Use the Outside Toilet) Lane'. Although 'Where's my Snorkle? (I Need to Use the Outside Toilet)' was a quite common expression in 18th Century Brighton, even before the floods.

At the end of the 18th Century, Brighton became fashionable thanks to the patronage of the Prince Regent. As many homes in the Old Town were demolished to make space for the Royal Pavilion, the Prince ordered his soldiers to build a new road for the displaced. A competition was held amongst them to choose a name for the new road, and it was duly named 'New Road'. Second place went to 'Tell Him Where to Stick his New Road Street'.

In the 1780s the Prince Regent began to spend heavily on drink and womanising, to the deep dismay of his wife, Caroline of Brunswick. Parliament soon passed an act to prevent the Prince of Wales wasting public funds on frippery and adultery, one which has been studiously ignored by every heir to the throne ever since.

When Queen Victoria came to the throne, the Pavilion became her favourite holiday home. However, in 1841, the London to Brighton Railway was built close by, and she ordered that whenever she was in residence, trains should stop outside the town until she left. Perhaps someone should tell Network Rail she's not still there.

It was in Victorian times that the writer Lewis Carroll regularly visited his sister in Brighton. He was inspired by watching his niece at play to write both *Alice's Adventures in Wonderland*, and *Alice's Adventures Doing Cartwheels for Uncle Lewis*.

It wasn't until the advent of cheap rail travel that Londoners began to flock to the city in their thousands, when Brighton became known as 'London by the Sea', much in the same way as nearby Eastbourne became known as 'Kick the Bucket by the Sea'.

Brighton was heavily bombed during World War II, but Adolf Hitler ordered that the Royal Pavilion should be left intact, as he intended to use it as a base following a successful invasion. Hitler held a particular affinity for the building, as it only had one ballroom.

Brighton's first modern shopping centre was built in the 1960s. Called 'Churchill Square', it was named in memory of the great wartime leader, and was modelled on his concrete bunker.

Brighton still shows evidence of the disastrous sea floods

Brighton's cultural heritage is well known, and never was the elegant seaside town more in the cultural spotlight than when it was immortalised unmistakably in Graham Greene's novel *Our Man in Havana*.

Proud of its heritage, Brighton City Council has taken to

naming its buses after local landmarks and people, such as the Boxer, Chris Eubank, the Devil's Dyke, Julie Burchill and a nice couple from Hove: Mr and Mrs Notinservice.

Other famous Brighton residents include Jordan and husband Peter Andre. Rumours abound that their marriage is in fact a sham, and the paparazzi are constantly trying to get photos of the pretend pair falling out.

Anita Roddick opened her first business in Brighton during the early 70s. She offered such alternative delights as 'jojoba and sesame oil', 'tea-tree bark with nettle extract', 'seaweed and willow-sap tincture', plus over thirty varieties of Brazilian tree frog creams. However, after six months the restaurant folded, and she went into skin care products instead.

Chris Eubank lives near Brighton in part of a converted monastery. He is often seen driving his famous truck, but ran into trouble recently when he was stopped by the police. By the time he'd finished giving his address – 'Sixty-seven, Cistercian House, Sheepshank Street, Shoreham, West Sussex' – he'd inadvertently drowned two traffic cops.

Sadly one of Brighton's great unsung heroes retired recently. Eighty-year-old Ted Latham was the town's longest serving deckchair attendant until August 2007, when he collapsed on the beach, and it took three people half an hour to put him back up again.

EASTBOURNE

ℵⴲℬ

ASTBOURNE is a popular seaside resort on what's known
as the Côte d'Azur of Sussex, 'côte' meaning 'coast'
and 'azur' meaning 'blue rinse'.

The earliest settlement in Eastbourne, on a stream (or
'bourne') had no name, but as the hamlet grew, a competition
was held to choose a title to suit this town to the east of the
bourne. On the day of final entries, Halley's comet passed over
and the new name became 'Bourne Under A Wanderin' Star'.
However, following copyright problems with the writers of *Paint
Your Wagon*, it was changed to 'Oklahoma'. This resulted in obvious confusion, with coach parties travelling to the American
Midwest in search of a bingo hall, and so the town became
'Eastbourne'.

Eastbourne grew rapidly as a garrison town during the
Napoleonic Wars, when troops were massed at the town to
embark for Waterloo. But as usual, the 8.45 stopping service was
cancelled, so they went to Belgium instead. There they met
Napoleon in the conflict which was to give the famous railway
station its name – the Battle of Maidstone West.

During Victorian times, Eastbourne's town centre was rebuilt under the Duke of Devonshire, who sent Henry Currey on
a tour of Europe to collect architectural ideas. Currey travelled
to Paris, Berlin and Pisa, the result being the fine neo-classical

construction in Grove Road known as 'The Leaning Wall of Eiffel'.

In 1847, a sporting academy was established at Devonshire Park to prepare English lady tennis players for Wimbledon. Training involved a single player hitting the ball against the side of the clubhouse, and every summer since, Eastbourne has echoed to the cry of 'advantage brick wall'.

It was in 1903 that Eastbourne came to the world's attention as the first town to create a municipal bus company running steam powered coaches. However, the people of Bexhill rioted in fear of such modern technology, when the service was extended there in 1997.

Eastbourne has long been the subject of Royal patronage, a connection specially commemorated during the Silver Jubilee when the Mayor, Winifred Lee, was presented to the Queen Mother. Most other towns just gave her a box of chocolates.

In the 1930s the young Princesses Elizabeth and Margaret holidayed in Eastbourne and built castles on the beach. However, these had to come down after they were refused planning permission on the grounds that the sisters already had seven between them.

Charles Darwin developed his theory of evolution in Eastbourne, and his great-great-great-great grandson still lives in the town, where he retired after a long career on television, appearing in adverts for PG Tips.

During World War II, Eastbourne became the first British town to be the target of a bombing raid, but with improvements in aircraft range, the RAF soon started hitting Germany instead. At the start of the war, many schoolchildren were evacuated to

The director of C4's Big Brother *setting camera angles for the first series*

Eastbourne from London, but being too close to the action, they were soon taken by train to Coventry.

Noted historic buildings in Eastbourne include the Old Manor House where recent restoration work has revealed a hidden wall mosaic and a priest-hole. But despite putting traps down, they haven't caught him yet.

Famous names associated with Eastbourne include Douglas Bader and the town's museum holds some of his personal possessions. These include his last school report which reads: 'in future, Bader really must learn to pull his socks up'.

Political thinkers Marx and Engels came to Eastbourne to

formulate their Communist Party Manifesto, but the pair fell out over whether it really was the workers' inalienable right to control the means of productivity, and so Marx instead opened a small underpants shop with his friend Spencer.

The composer Debussy, inspired by the view from his balcony, wrote his orchestral work 'La Mer' at Eastbourne's Grand Hotel. The following year he returned but, being allocated a room without a sea view, wrote his less popular piece, 'La Tesco's Carpark'.

A regular summer visitor to Eastbourne was the writer Richmal Crompton, who was responsible for bringing us the amusing little character, Martin Jarvis.

With its close proximity to France, these days Eastbourne is a popular summer choice for students on school shoplifting exchanges.

HASTINGS

⬠⬡⬢

ASTINGS is an historic coastal town with much to be commended. The story of Hastings only really begins with the famous battle, which was fought at a nearby town called 'Battle'. Now what are the chances of that happening?

In September 1066, William the Conqueror assembled his army across the Channel, and set sail with his army of 9,000 Normans after one of the most confusing roll-calls ever taken.

William landed at nearby Pevensey Bay, where legend has it that as he climbed from his boat, he fell into the water. His apprehensive troops considered this a bad omen, but William grabbed a handful of shingle and called out: 'Look, I have taken England already'. It was with a sense of great relief that his entire force immediately began to paddle furiously back across the Channel.

Having been called back for their second attempt, and with news of the landing spreading, the Saxon King Harold marched his men from Stamford Bridge, where after a long drawn-out struggle, they'd beaten Hardrada's Norwegians on penalty shoot-outs.

Harold's army was something of a ramshackle force, largely comprised of farmers intent on driving the invaders back by putting up signs that read: 'Private Land – Keep Out'.

The battle took place around Senlac Hill, and after a full day's fighting, the English were defeated and King Harold was struck in the eye by an arrow. He was carried to the Hastings Free Hospital where he was pronounced 'dead', and from there to a fee paying one, where his condition was upgraded to 'alive'.

William then set about building the castle we see today and first awarded the area to a fellow warrior, Odo, Duke of Alençon, whom William treated as the younger brother he never had, much to the irritation of the younger brother he did have.

In the years following the invasion, Sussex was split into fiefdoms or 'sees', as they were known, and the 'see' of Hastings passed into the control of Bishop Ralph le Bon. Sadly, the town serfs refused to take his rule seriously, after he renamed the keep 'le Bon See Castle'.

As you would expect, Hastings' local history is inextricably linked with the sea. In 1067, Hastings joined with Romney, Hythe, Dover and Sandwich to form a brotherhood of coastal towns. Intended to defend England from any cross-channel invasion, they took the crest of a running horse rampant and stable door bolted. This Cinque Ports League still exists today, but recently changed its name to the Vauxhall Conference.

In the 20th Century, Hastings became notable as the birthplace of television, as its inventor Logie Baird lived in the town with his companion Boo-Boo. The Scottish engineer spent several years in Hastings developing the very first TV set, intended as a relaxation tool to take workers' minds off the daily grind of cooking, household repairs and gardening.

SOUTHSEA

ℵ⚛ℬ

S OUTHSEA is often overlooked in favour of its more famous neighbour, Portsmouth, but as Portsmouth is a lively, bustling city dripping with a rich history, that comes as no surprise.

The great pioneering civil engineer, Isambard Kingdom Brunel, was born in Portsmouth and was christened in the local church amid great celebration, as his parents had just won the first two prizes in Southsea's 'most stupid novelty name for a small child' competition.

As you might expect of a community with such long associations with the sea, Southsea offers interested visitors the opportunity to seek out many museums replicating how a simple island race used to live in the distant past. Alternatively, if they want to see how a simple island race still does live in the distant past, they can nip on a ferry over to the Isle of Wight.

Southsea is in effect the residential district of Portsmouth and owes its prosperity to Portsmouth's thriving marine industry. This first arose after Henry VIII built a dry dock in the city's port. However it wasn't really dry in those days. That didn't happen until ownership passed to Southern Water PLC.

Most famously, Portsmouth is associated with Lord Nelson's flagship, the *Victory*, to which visitors flock to see the very spot where the great man fell. It's marked by a brass plaque reading:

'At this spot on July 12th 1789, Admiral Horatio Nelson tripped over a bloke screwing a brass plaque to the deck, after inadvertently putting his patch on the wrong eye.'

*As glass hit record highs on the commodities markets,
there was a spate of window thefts in Southsea*

CHICHESTER

☙✠☙

CHICHESTER is often overlooked in favour of its more famous neighbour, Southsea, but as Southsea is a lively, bustling city dripping with a rich history, that comes as no surprise.

In the 4th Century AD a settlement was founded in Chichester by the Roman XXXIIIVVV Legion, the famous 'fighting Redoubtable Stutterers', who were actually supposed to found Chester.

In the late 16th Century, Arab dhows plying cargoes of exotic spices along the Red Sea coast down the Horn of Africa and into Zanzibar, sought another entrepot from which to trade precious stones with white slavers and the tribes of the Serengeti. Luckily they discovered Dar Es Salaam, so didn't ever get as far as Chichester.

Chichester grew streadily from the Middle Ages and today is a market town centred around just four main streets: North Street, South Street, East Street and West Street. Originally there were more, but they were pulled down as too many visiting merchants became hopelessly lost. The city guidebook of 1423 advises that to reach the town centre from the harbour: '. . . go North up South Street, turn East along West Street, then South along North-West Street and West into South-East Street before turning North again along South-by-South-West Street into West-by-South-West Street, taking care to ignore North-East-by-South-West-by-East-North-East-by-West-East Street which is a dead end, and then it's first on your left.'

The 1981 Glorious Goodwood race meeting was spoiled by the appearance of a male streaker

ENGLAND
THE SOUTH-WEST

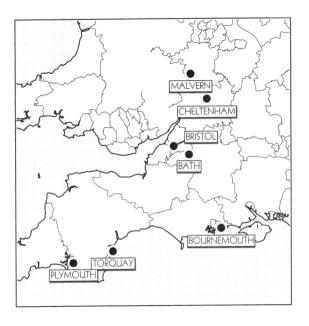

Gloucestershire, summer 2007.
The government's emergency flood defence
measures prove every bit as successful as expected

CHELTENHAM

སྒྲུ

C HELTENHAM is a fascinating city with a fine history. Originally a small Cotswold village, this spa town first found favour during the fashionable Regency period. This was largely due to the patronage of Arthur Wellesley, the Duke of Wellington (who popularised his eponymous footwear in Cheltenham), Lord Sandwich (who brought the leading convenience item food that bears his name), and Viscount Picnic (who introduced the two). Their alfresco social gatherings were invariably also graced by Alfred Thermos, third Earl of Bovril, and Sir Jonathan Annoying-Wasp.

Every March, racegoers gather at Cheltenham to enjoy the world famous Gold Cup, which was originally run over hurdles by four-year-old Arabs. Nowadays of course, they use horses.

And nearby is that acme of educational establishments, Cheltenham Ladies' College. It is important to recall that Tim Brooke-Taylor's mother, Rachel 'Ray' Pawson*, used to teach gymnastics there, partly because of her unstinting services to the promotion of physical training, but mainly because a gratuitous mention of her name might result in an extra copy of this book being sold.

* Rachel Frances Pawson, daughter of Frank Pawson, England's centre forward in the 1880s. She herself was also a lacrosse international.

MALVERN

MALVERN is a fine town boasting much of interest to the visitor. The town nestles in the Malvern Hills under the Worcestershire Beacon. After climbing to the summit, many hikers gaze out across fourteen counties, and under certain weather conditions it is possible to catch a sight of Birmingham, despite the many, clearly-posted warning signs.

The name 'Malvern' derives from the Celtic words describing the original settlement. The prefix 'Mall' means 'spring water pools', while the word 'Vern' refers to small areas of woodland. Hence the precise translation: 'Little Wood's Pools'.

Malvern is of course most famous for the purity of its natural spring waters which are bottled and exported worldwide. The still variety is prized as a curative for such ailments as excessive flatulence, while the sparkling variety is famous for remedying a lack of it.

Malvern's proud boast is that theirs is the only natural spring water used by Queen Elizabeth II. And when in 1987 A Royal Act of Charter was drawn up to sanction supplies of bottled water to Her Majesty, she kindly invited the town council to witness as she passed it.

The town's first known documentation dates from 1083, when its lavish Benedictine Monastery was built. It's recorded that this was the cause of much friction with the nearby Convent of St Agatha, as the monastery was maintained by a generous endowment from Edward the Confessor, and the nuns jealously eyed the monks who were obviously so well endowed.

Famous names associated with the area include Sir Edward Elgar. It was in Malvern that he composed his *Enigma Variations*, which later found great commercial stage success as *Bletchley Park, the Musical.*

The nearby public school, Malvern College, was founded in 1862. This was taken over during World War II by the Air Ministry, as a research base exploiting advances in microwave technology to develop an aircraft tracking radar system. Expected to take many months of development, they actually managed it in just two and half minutes. As a result, air defences could readily identify and bring down Luftwaffe bombers, the aircraft being hit by a barrage of piping-hot, ready-cooked pigeons.

Famous old boys of Malvern College include the occultist Alastair Crowley, and it was while at Malvern that he first became interested in Black Magic, the paranormal and re-incarnation. Crowley was buried in St Wulfrun's churchyard in 1934, at Golders Green Synagogue in 1956, and finally in 1972, at the West Dudley pet cemetery.

Another notable grave at St Wulfrun's is that of Britain's first recorded fatal case of asbestosis. The poor chap was buried there in 1827, but not until after they'd spent three weeks trying to cremate him.

The ancient county of Worcestershire has much to admire, including Hagley Hall, the family seat of the Lyttelton dynasty. Set in 350 acres of superbly landscaped deer park, the house contains Van Dyke masterpieces and fine Chippendale furniture. The land, house and title have passed down the line to my cousin, Viscount Cobham, the 8th Lord Lyttelton and his heirs, meaning that at any given time I am but one, small, and entirely fatal minibus accident away from wealth, privilege and sublime indolence beyond my wildest dreams.

Hagley Hall (second gardener's potting shed)

A world famous local product is of course Worcestershire sauce. The first reference dates from the English Civil War, when Oliver Cromwell proudly proclaimed to Parliament that he had won the Bottle of Worcester, thanks to drawing Yellow 61 in that year's 'Roundhead Social Club Raffle'. It was in 1835 that the famous dark and spicy condiment was discovered by two chemists: Lea and Perrins. Their ingredients remain a closely guarded secret even today, known only to a handful of members of the Lea and Perrins families, and anyone who can be bothered to read the label marked 'ingredients' on the side of the bottle.

BRISTOL

ℬⅅℬ

BRISTOL is a fine city boasting a rich history and culture. The town originally grew as a port, and it was from Bristol in 1497 that John Cabot set off to find a new route to the Spice Islands by sailing north west. He instead discovered a strange, hostile world which he named 'Newfoundland', until the natives explained that they actually called it 'Swansea'.

Later, Cabot set sail for Canada and began trading with the natives. The North American Indians gave his men fine jewellery of opals mounted in gold and silver, buffalo furs to make warm clothing, and quality tobacco leaf to be traded in Europe's markets, while in return, Cabot and his men gave them smallpox.

Subsequent trading links were established with the Nordic countries: from Denmark came cured bacon, Norway provided salted herring, while Iceland supplied frozen peas and three-for-two packets of chicken nuggets.

With the Atlantic trade came grey squirrels, which have driven out the native red variety and overrun the whole of England except the Isle of Wight. Arriving in Bristol from America, the grey squirrel has the Latin name 'Sciurus Carolensis'. As it will be unfamiliar to the population of the Isle of Wight, it should be explained that America is a big country over the water. No doubt I'll be getting letters from islanders about that comment – just as soon as their postman has rowed to the mainland.

Bristol's prosperity was further assured by the spoils of the slave trade. This murky history is commemorated in the Bristol and Transatlantic Slavery Gallery, where visitors can experience what it was like to be herded into an overcrowded, stinking hulk to be terrorized by the crew. Alternatively, they can book a Ryanair flight.

In its heyday, Bristol's dock area was known for its many taverns, and it was in one of these that Daniel Defoe met Alexander Selkirk. Over many hours, during a long evening of ales and porters, Selkirk regaled Defoe with his endless stories. It was this meeting that inspired Defoe to write his most famous novel: *How I Had My Arse Bored Off By a Drunken Scotsman in Bristol*.

Defoe later went on to write *Robinson Crusoe*, based on Selkirk's story of being stranded on a desert island with the company of just one other human, whom he named 'Kirsty Young'. That wasn't the native's real name of course, but Selkirk could hardly write in his diary that a big bloke called 'Friday' was his right hand for thirty years. The story comes to a thrilling and completely unpredictable climax, when a large wave threatens to wash away Crusoe's record collection and he has to decide which one to save, even though there are only eight of them and he could just as easily pick them all up.

Bristol is rightly proud of its association with Isambard Kingdom Brunel, who is celebrated for creating SS Great Britain, the UK branch of the German ex-servicemen's club. Brunel also designed the Clifton Suspension Bridge.

Completed in 1864, locals were amazed to see construction workers hanging over the side in baskets, high above the gorge, and it was later decided they'd look better planted with geraniums.

The project ran out of money and had to be completed using second-hand chains. It's not known where they came from, but it is recorded that as one was being pulled through the south tower, the River Avon flushed out to sea.

In Brunel's time, clocks in Bristol and the West Country were between ten and twenty minutes behind London, but with the coming of the railway, these had to be regularised. Some towns refused to comply, however, and to this day when it's 12 noon in London, in Weston-Super-Mare it's still 1963.

The city of Bristol is rightly proud of its architectural heritage. Nestling on College Green is found Bristol Cathedral, which is Britain's finest example of a 'Hall Church', and is noted for its stained glass, although it's nothing a quick rub over with Windolene won't fix.

The original building was founded in 1140 by Robert Fitzharding, ancestor to the Earls of Berkeley. It was this family that later formed the famous Berkeley Hunt, whose activities have recently been curtailed by legislation banning rhyming slang.

Bristol's modern history is very much associated with aviation. In 1910, Britain's first commercial aircraft factory was established at nearby Filton, to manufacture the Bristol Boxkite. Despite the Boxkite's limited range, commercial flights soon began, with routes going as far as the string would stretch. However, services were eventually cancelled when passengers became tired of having to climb out of a tall tree after every landing.

Filton had particular associations with the Concorde project. With a transatlantic flight time of a little over three hours, it was the proud boast of British Airways that Concorde passengers could have their breakfast in London, their lunch in New York and their luggage in Uzbekistan.

The Barry Manilow Memorial, Filton

In the 1950s, the factory turned to making luxury cars such as the Bristol Bulldog and the Bristol 401, which still have an enthusiastic following today. Every summer, the Owners' Club meets to display their classic vehicles. And while they chat and swap stories, members' wives proudly clean and polish their Bristols, which are then displayed and judged by the Mayor.

Well-known names associated with Bristol include the infamous Judge Jeffreys, who presided over the Bloody Assizes. Jeffreys drank heavily to dull a painful condition, and took little notice of defence pleas. During one notorious session, 233 persons were hanged, drawn, quartered and gibbeted in the market place, before Mrs Jeffreys pointed out that he'd inadvertently executed all the guests at his birthday party.

The sculptor, Edward Hodges Bailey was born in Bristol in 1788. He is best known for his 16-foot figure of Lord Nelson, a project which, after two years of stone carving, was nearly a disaster, when Bailey slipped and knocked the right arm off. He was just about to start all over again, when, by a wonderful stroke of luck, news came that Nelson had had the same limb ripped off by a cannon ball.

It was the local Liberal MP Samuel Plimsoll who introduced the Merchant Shipping Act of 1876, which required every vessel to be painted with a Plimsoll Line to regulate the safe loading of gym shoes.

These days, several famous names make Bristol their home, including the television actor Tony Robinson, who is best known as the scruffy idiot sidekick in *Time Team*.

Another resident is Paul McGann, from the famous actor family which includes his brothers: Joe, Mark and Renault.

BATH

༖ⴟ༖

BATH is a fascinating town with a fine history. The city was originally called Aquae Sulis because of its spa, and visitors can still see the partial remains of a system of hot and cold water pipes begun by Roman plumbing engineers in 54 AD. They returned to their depot in Verulamium in 53 AD to fetch parts and, despite a promise to return the following Thursday, haven't been seen since. However, they did leave the town with a unique legacy and a call-out fee of seventy quid pro quo.

Amongst other attractions is the nearby Royal Pump Room, housing a fine display of royal pumps. Next to that is the Regency Trainer House, just along from the Queen Anne flip-flop archive.

Apart from the natural hot springs, intrepid tourists who seek something different might do worse than head for the Norwegian quarter of the town, with its many ethnic bistros serving traditional Scandinavian cuisine. After enjoying a dinner of wild elk and smorgasbord, washed down with pewter goblets of whale blubber mead, they may care to wander by the river and help celebrate the Festival of the Burning Longship, when fierce bearded locals don horned helmets and wave mighty battle swords as they chant in praise of their Lord of Valhalla. Anyone who visits Bath and misses this colourful and dramatic event, will kick themselves when they realise they should have gone to Reykjavik.

BOURNEMOUTH

☒⚙☒

THE DELIGHTFUL Dorset town of Bournemouth was developed into the resort we know today in the 1890s, when fine drives and avenues were laid out to be opened by Queen Victoria and visiting guest Kaiser Wilhelm, in full military garb. At the ceremony, everyone gasped in amazement, except Kaiser Wilhelm, who gasped because he'd inadvertently sat on his hat.

The town's origins can be traced to one Lewis Tregonwell, who built the first house in Bournemouth in 1810 as a retirement home. He planted the famous pine trees of the area for their scent, which was believed to cure various diseases. The habit of tree sniffing has lately fallen out of fashion, with the advent of pine fresh toilet duck. Tregonwell lived to be 107, when the town went into mourning at the loss of their founding father at such a tender age.

When Kaiser Wilhelm came to Bournemouth, his visit was sponsored by Schmidt's Automated Anti-Dandruff Shoulder Brushes

In the early years of Bournemouth, shops were banned and tradesmen had to call from Poole or Christchurch. It was only thanks to the townsfolk's exceptionally acute sense of hearing that anyone ever heard them at all.

It wasn't until 1941 that Bournemouth came to the world's attention, when the course of World War II was changed for good, after the Japanese made the mistake of bombing Poole Harbour.

Nearby is Brownsea Island, where, in 1907, Lord Baden Powell founded the Boy Scout Movement. Ever since, young lads have gained their merit badges in camping and field craft by reference to his *Scouting For Boys*, and fire-starting by reference to his *Arson For Beginners*.

Bournemouth residents are proud to show visitors the region's ancient sedimentary beds from the Miocene era, although for extra comfort they might prefer the new orthopaedic beds from Slumberland.

Dorset's most remarkable attraction is the Cerne Abbas Giant, a graphic representation of a naked man cut into the chalk hillside. Many people join the distinguished Cerne Abbas Society, and each May Day the society marches through the town, led by its longest standing member.

PLYMOUTH

৪৫৪

PLYMOUTH is a fascinating city with a fine history. Now a leading port, Plymouth is first recorded in cave drawings by local Celts when they noticed an Iron Age tribe had arrived there to mine ore and smelt in a basic fashion, but to be fair this was before the invention of bathrooms.

From this small settlement grew the major port of Wessex, the Saxon kingdom that evolved into England, and for a short time Plymouth was its capital city. But everyone soon got fed up with lousy public transport, not talking to each other and paying nearly four quid for a pint of weak lager, and decided to let London have a go instead.

Probably Plymouth's most celebrated son is Sir Francis Drake. Sailing for the Caribbean in 1577, Drake and his men fought their way up through a hundred leagues of the Spanish Main, ending a solid season as runners-up in Division Two. When Drake returned home in triumph the following year, the delighted townsfolk swarmed out to greet him, dancing all the way from St Andrew's Cross to the famous Plymouth Sound, an R and B derived genre not dissimilar to the later Mersey Beat but with more bass-driven riffs.

It was from Plymouth that the Pilgrim Fathers set sail in 1620. Before boarding the *Mayflower*, these devout Puritans held a service of thanksgiving at the Plymouth Hoe, followed by hymns at the Exeter Shovel and prayers for the Torquay Rotary Mower.

Their crossing was eventful and even saw the birth of a baby to Master and Mistress Hopkins. Inspired by the vast expanse of the Atlantic, they named the boy 'Oceanus Freedom Hopkins'. By coincidence, exactly the same thing happened during a commemorative voyage in 1987, and what joy there was amongst the crew at the christening of 'Oil Slick Condom Johnson'.

Later, Captain Cook sailed from Plymouth for Tahiti on government service in search of the Transit of Venus. Those were the days when you could rely on the authorities to recover a stolen motor vehicle.

After six months in the then little known South Pacific, Cook's crew mutinied in protest at his constant rendition of 'There is Nothing Like a Dame'. Cook then sailed on for seven years, braving storms and hostile natives to navigate beyond the known world, securing Australia for Britain for the purpose of guaranteeing her an unlimited supply of TV soaps and cheap but over-cheerful bar staff.

In 1974, the Tour de France visited Plymouth. It wasn't planned but the cyclists were so drugged up they overshot going up the Cherbourg Peninsula, cleared the Channel and landed in Devon

TORQUAY

ॐ֍ॐ

TORQUAY, the Queen of the English Riviera, owes its very existence to tourism and has much to offer the interested visitor, including Kent's Cavern. It was in these caves that archaeologists unearthed Britain's earliest evidence of human habitation from the Neolithic Age, including a rudimentary toilet consisting of a prehistoric hole in the ground. And that's not the area's only connection with France.

The modern town owes its expansion to the Napoleonic Wars, when Torbay was developed as a naval base. Admiral Lord Nelson was hospitalised in Torquay after losing an eye at the Battle of the Nile, and it was in Torquay that he famously remarked to his surgeons: 'I'd give my right arm to have that eye back'. One can only imagine Nelson's fury when he came round to discover that as he didn't have a right arm, they'd removed his left one.

In 1815, Napoleon himself was brought to Torquay on his way into exile. He was billeted with his guards at a local inn for a short while, and it was after this that he sent a note that read: 'Not to-night Josephine, I've just been forced to spend the night in the Duke of Wellington'.

In Victorian times, Torquay's climate was known for its restorative properties, and the town became a Mecca for the sick and ailing, twice hosting the World Latin American Scabies Championship.

The famous Café de Paris, Torquay. The 'fin de siècle' art nouveau interior is based on the famous Café de Torquay, Paris

One famous convalescent visitor to Torquay was the Victorian poet and critic Elizabeth Barrett Browning, and it's the town's proud boast that it was in Torquay that she invented gravy.

The splendid Oldways Mansion was built at nearby Paignton by Isaac Singer, the American-born industrialist and sewing-machine magnate. His son further developed the family's home and, as an early manufacturer of domestic freezers, became known as the world's first fridge magnate.

Rudyard Kipling also lived at Paignton and there wrote his immortal lines: 'If you can keep your head when all about you are losing theirs, then why not treat yourself to one of my exceedingly good cakes.'

The town was also the home in Victorian times of one Josiah Nesbitt, who tried to promote himself as a fairground attraction as England's tallest dwarf. At five foot six and half inches, he was overshadowed by his five foot seven brother Amos, who quite remarkably claimed to be the country's shortest giant. They found little success, until they teamed up to tour with Jolly Jim Spragg, the world's chattiest hermit, Agnes Peach, the world's least tattooed lady, and 'Gunfire' Freddie, 'The Human Melon Ball', who defied death nightly by sitting in a bowl of syrup.

According to the official town tourist guide, at nearby Babbacombe is found the country's largest miniature model village. Not, one would think, a great boast.

Another popular local attraction is the Spanish Barn, which housed prisoners captured from the Armada. Many of these settled in the Torquay area and their descendants can still be seen working by night in the many local tapas bars, and by day in the town square beating a donkey to death with sticks.

Wimpey Homes' new housing estate, Babbacombe

In the 18th Century, the local coastline became the notorious haunt of smugglers, who constantly evaded capture to the irritation of customs officers. Contraband would be unloaded and carried under cover of darkness from nearby Smugglers' Cove, via Smugglers' Alley, to be stored in the cellar of the Smuggler's Inn. If only those customs men had had more to go on.

Probably Torquay's most famous daughter was the author and playwright: Agatha Christie. Her stage drama, *The Mousetrap*, has been running continuously in the West End of London since 1952, but in those days they did tend to write much longer plays. *The Mousetrap* was actually adapted from Christie's radio drama, *Three Blind Mice*, but the title was later changed as everyone quickly worked out that it was the farmer's wife who did it, with a carving knife.

ENGLAND
THE HOME COUNTIES

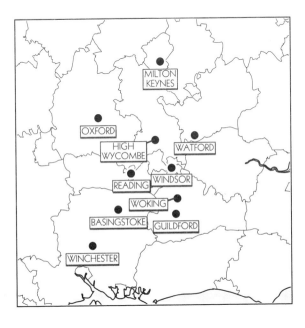

MILTON
KEYNES

OXFORD

HIGH
WYCOMBE

WATFORD

READING

WINDSOR

WOKING

BASINGSTOKE

GUILDFORD

WINCHESTER

WOKING

ᘒᑲᗴ

THE FINE SOUTH England town of Woking is described by no less an authority than the Longer OED as: 'A town in southern England'.

As you might expect, Woking revels in a fascinating history. It was in 1587 that Vasco Da Gama set sail in search of trade routes, and his vessel was blown off course into a broad river estuary. Trekking inland for several days, Da Gama came upon a small settlement and claimed it for King Ferdinand of Portugal. This is what we now call the Amazon Basin. But just think. If only he'd turned right instead of left coming out of Lisbon, Woking could so easily now be the capital of Brazil.

Old Woking is first mentioned in the Domesday Book, when the Normans arrived at what was then a hunting heath, noted for its trade in animal skins. When their new rulers came to buy pelts, the local Saxons are recorded as helpfully putting up signs directing all visiting Norman barons in the direction of the fur queue.

In the 16th Century, Henry VIII was a frequent visitor to Woking Palace, whom he saw beat West Bromwich Albion two-nil in a thrilling cup-tie in 1536.

John Donne spent some time nearby on the Wey Navigation Canal, where he wrote *Fear Not for Whom the Bell Tolls* in between presenting his marvellous Radio Two programme.

Modern Woking is famously home to the Kenwood Mixer,

named after its inventor Ken Woodmixer. Life was transformed for a generation of young 1960s' housewives experiencing the joys of its electrically induced pulse mechanism, and as a bonus it chopped food as well.

The town guide tells us that Woking's environs are famous for their wildlife habitats, home to rare types of bee, adders and the unique spider-hunting wasp. Sadly, the Woking & District Wasp Pack have recently had their spider hunt disrupted by saboteurs, laying false trails of jam sandwiches.

In 1994 the Spice Girls started their sensational pop careers at Woking's Knaphill Studio. It was on 17th July that five unknown but supremely talented female vocalists were booked in there for a recording session, so the Spice Girls had to wait.

Other famous names associated with the area include the Formula One team McLaren and the writer of *War of the Worlds*, H. G. Wells. Proud Woking commemorated these local success stories by erecting a huge racing car and a seventeen-metre statue of a martian. One can only imagine the relief felt by the council when they missed out on leasing premises to the Viagra corporation.

The prototype Kenwood mixer proved a little unwieldy

GUILDFORD

ॐⲪॐ

I T'S NOT EVERY Surrey commuter town that can boast not only a bustling Bohemian Latin Quarter but also a Moorish citadel surrounded by a warren of dark sinister streets that provided film locations for Truffaut, Fassbinder and Bergman, and neither can Guildford.

The town of Guildford nestles on the North Downs, the ridge of hills formed during the Tertiary Period when they were attached to what are now the Swiss Alps. This ancient connection is still reflected at Guildford's annual festival of cuckoo clocks, chocolate and Nazi-looted fine art.

The town is first recorded in the 9th Century when King Alfred used Guildford as a base to launch his attack on Danish-held London, his army managing to reach the outskirts of the capital in less than six hours; a feat occasionally matched to this day by South West Trains.

The name Guildford derives from the old English 'Golden Ford' and when a new town was recently built nearby, tradition

Cuckoo clocks being lubricated with earwax, Guildford

dictated it should be named in similar fashion and so became 'Little Metallic Bronze Datsun on the Down'.

Guildford really began to grow after the construction of the Wey Navigation Canal, providing 19th Century merchants a means to distribute their products and 20th Century consumers somewhere to dump their old ones.

In 1837, one Josiah Hawkins came to Guildford and built England's first ever paper mill. Sadly, during the Great Gale of 1838, it blew away.

Nearby are many natural attractions, including Surrey's highest point at Leith Hill. Allowing for weather conditions, on a reasonable day you can see as far as Orpington. On a perfect day you can't see it all.

The town is also noted as the burial place of Lewis Carroll, the professor of mathematics who wrote three classic novels: *Alice in Wonderland* and *Alice Through the Looking Glass*. Visiting his grave now, one might wonder where one would ever find a Looking Glass Wonderland today. Well, good news! There's one on the South Circular between PC World and Allied Carpets.

Lewis Carroll's grave. Note the inscription 'Fell asleep January 14th 1898'. Later the law was changed to make it illegal to bury dozing relatives

WINCHESTER

℘⚙℘

WINCHESTER is a fine city set at the heart of the ancient kingdom of Wessex. The area was originally inhabited by early Britons during the Bronze Age, when they made fine jewellery and tools. With the advent of the Iron Age, improved swords and arrowheads could be fashioned, but when the Ice Age arrived, they found frozen water a poor material for making weapons.

It was the Romans who established a town in Winchester on the site of a small British settlement and called it 'Wenta Belgarum'. The Latin word 'wenta' simply meant 'home', while the word 'belgarum' indicated a base of rocky hills or 'tors'. Hence the literal translation: 'Home Base Tors'.

With the withdrawal of the Romans, the town went into decline until revived as a Saxon stronghold to fend off the Vikings. Much of England to the north-west was terrorised by invading Danes, who forced the native populace to endure such hardships as pillage, slavery, torture and flat-pack kitchen units.

Under the rule of Alfred the Great, Winchester became the capital city of England. Alfred reunited the kingdom in the face of Danish invasion and became known as the father of the English navy, as he had several dozen girlfriends in Portsmouth. It is recorded that Alfred was buried in Winchester in the year 899. However, later historical research has revealed that Alfred didn't actually die until 901, so that must have been a traumatic couple of years for the poor man.

With the city constantly expanding, St John's Hospital was built in Winchester in 935 AD. Their first ever patient is recorded as one Wil the Shepherd. His descendants still live in the area and treasure the document confirming his admission date, which has been passed down the family since the very day it was received, in 1984. St John's is believed to be the oldest medieval hospital in Britain. The NHS recently began a modernisation programme to bring all their others up to this standard.

With the building of the cathedral, the city became a venue for Royal weddings. In 1002, Emma, the daughter of the Duke of Normandy, came to Winchester to marry Ethelred the Unready, who used the occasion to launch his unsuccessful range of torch batteries.

By 1900 the mighty cathedral was subsiding and major repair work was required to its foundations. Reconstruction work was supervised by one Francis Fox, who was working on the London Underground. Luckily he was able to fit them in, as he only ever turned up to drive on the Northern Line two days a week. Investigation revealed the substructure had suffered a major fracture, but excavation holes constantly flooded with water. Fox therefore employed a diver called William Walker, whom he supervised with shouts of 'Mind the gap'.

The cathedral is today a major attraction and houses the 12th Century Winchester Bible, which is beautifully illuminated. This Christmas they're hoping to get Ainsley Harriott to switch it on.

Another famous name with local associations is that of Jane

Austen, who is pictured in the city's portrait gallery with her hair in a bun. That was the evidence that got her sacked from the Winchester Grill Burger Bar.

BASINGSTOKE

℘Ժ℘

THE HAMPSHIRE TOWN of Basingstoke boasts an historical tapestry richly woven with culture. Evidence of an early settlement and its trading links may be seen at the town's Willis Museum, which houses Roman pottery found at Silchester camp and a hoard of bronze and iron European coins, retrieved from Basingstoke's parking meters.

Pride of place in the town's museum goes to the skull of a 300,000-year-old male, discovered locally in 1962. A primitive being with short legs and long arms, 'Basingstoke Man' is described by experts as genetically somewhere between ape and human. Sadly they don't know anything about that old skull.

The name 'Basingstoke' is first mentioned when William the Conqueror commissioned the Domesday Book, where it is described as a settlement with a population of some 200-odd people, but then the Normans could be a bit judgmental.

The result of Britain's first experiment into genetic modification holding a large marrow

Basingstoke's early prosperity was based on the production of wool. Sheep were raised locally, and their wool was cleaned by being beaten with a mixture of water and clay by large wooden hammers driven by watermills. Later, in a more enlightened age, it was decided to shear the sheep first.

Basingstoke's first hospital was founded in the early 13th Century and dedicated to St John the Baptist. However, medical treatment was crude in the extreme with amputations performed using a large, blunt axe, although a sharp one could be made available if you went private.

Basingstoke saw its ultimate test with The Black Death of 1347, which left the town decimated. ''Tis a sight to vex the spirit: Them the Lord hath spared do move with hollow cheeks and eyes that are sunken unto their sockets. Broken are they with despair and the pity of their existence. A stillness most dreadful and ghostly doth cloak the whole town withal', but other than those comments, the RAC Guide gives it two rosettes.

In 1392 the town was destroyed by fire and had to be completely rebuilt. The king subsequently made the 'good men' of Basingstoke into a corporation, giving them the right to use his common seal, as the sensitive nostrils of amphibious mammals made them useful as smoke alarms.

1657 saw the Basingstoke Witch Trials, where a woman named Goody Turner was found guilty of practising witchcraft. After surviving a ducking in the pond, an angry mob then tried to burn her at the stake, but she was too damp and kept going out. While they were drying her off, she asked for seventeen burglaries, two serious assaults and one attempted murder to be taken into account, so her sentence was reduced to community service.

Nearby is the home of the Dukes of Wellington since 1817, where visitors can see the grave of the first Duke's stallion, Copenhagen. It was after the Battle of Waterloo, where Wellington famously spent 18 hours in the saddle, that a grateful nation gave him his country seat – although he couldn't use it for at least a fortnight. Copenhagen was buried at Stratfield Saye House with full military honours. The grave is marked by a simple headstone and four hooves sticking out of the ground.

Jane Austen lived at nearby Steventon, and during her time there started a romance with a Basingstoke man, widely believed to be a forester, but their engagement lasted only one night. History doesn't record what suddenly prompted her to leave Acorn Willy Jenkins.

One of Basingstoke's most famous sons is Thomas Burberry, inventor of rain-proof gabardine. He perfected his proofing method after noticing that an oily substance from wool made a shepherd's trousers water resistant after prolonged contact with sheep. And it must have taken a mighty inventive brain to witness that sight and think about raincoats.

Famous names associated with Basingstoke include Hollywood movie star Elizabeth Hurley, who as a young girl was born and educated in the town. Her primary school teacher recalls Elizabeth taking her first acting lesson, and having seen her many films, the pupils were keen to invite her back for a second one.

The family of Sarah, Duchess of York, came from the nearby village of Dummer, which is presumably why she is constantly referred to as 'one of the Dummer Fergusons'.

Another Royal connection is that of Arthur Nash, official broom maker to Her Majesty the Queen, who lives in Basingstoke. Her Majesty doesn't believe in modern contrivances such as vacuum cleaners, when carpets can be cleaned perfectly well simply by ringing a small bell.

*Eton, 1936, shortly after a small hole appeared in the wall
of the adjoining Nurses' Home changing rooms*

WINDSOR

ଓఉ౫

WINDSOR gave its name to a type of chair, a knot and most famously, a soup, although this was before the Royal Borough changed its name from 'Campbell's Cream of Mushroom-on-Thames'.

But a stone's throw across the river is Eton, with its world-renowned school. A browse through the school records reveal that: 'famous Old Etonians include the Duke of Wellington, William Gladstone, George Orwell and Humphrey Lyttelton, the jazz musician and panel game chairman'. Curiously they don't record what the other three were famous for.

Windsor has a proud association with the Royal Family. It was in 1917 that the house of Saxe-Coburg-Gotha took their new name from the place where they loved to spend so much of their time. By the same tradition, when the young Sarah Ferguson married Prince Andrew, she naturally assumed the title 'Duchess of Airport'.

For the finest view of Windsor Castle it is best approached

HEATHROW TERMINAL 5

A family enjoys the third week of their holiday, summer 2008

through 'Henry VIII's Gateway', which thanks to a recent merger, is now officially known as 'Henry VIII's Budgens'.

A short journey out of town takes you to Windsor Safari Park, where if you're lucky, you might glimpse a pride of lions in search of wildebeest migrating south across the vast plains of the Thames Valley. You might also like to pay a visit to the successful new 'Legoland' theme park next door. For a small fee, parents can take their children to enjoy a large area of toy buildings constructed out of plastic bricks. Alternatively, they can save their money and take the kids to Milton Keynes for the day.

Windsor, where organic products, including banana oil car-wax, were developed

READING

ᛒᚠᛉ

EADING is a fine town steeped in a rich history. When the Norman King Henry I's body was returned from battle in France, his remains were buried at nearby Reading Abbey, although his heart was buried at Rheims, his eyes and tongue at Calais, while his bowels remained at Rouen, although that was put down to a dodgy frog-leg fritter.

The novelist Jane Austen was educated in Reading's Abbey School, and while her mythical Northanger Abbey is widely accepted by literary experts to be based on Reading Abbey, this is disputed, mainly by the Northangrian monks of Northanger Abbey at nearby Northanger.

William Laud, Archbishop of Canterbury from 1633, was born in Broad Street, where WH Smith stands, which is evidenced by the Laud family crest of a crossed pen and pencil set argent, topped by Readers' Wives rampant.

Britain's oldest known song was written in Reading in about 1240. Its Early English title: 'Sooma is icoomen in, lhooda sing cukku', which to our modern ear sounds quite meaningless, actually translates as 'Agadoo, doo, doo, push pineapple, shake the tree'.

Reading was also the birthplace of William Fox Talbot, who brought photography to the masses. His portrait was recently restored and hangs in the Reading Gallery, complete with a little sticker in the corner pointing out where the artist inadvertently left his thumb over the canvas.

Visitors may wish to take in the memorial to John Blagrave, the eminent 19th Century mathematician and 'father of Algebra', although, after being ribbed at school, little Algebra later changed his name on the advice of his aunt, Mrs Emily Quadratic-Equation.

World fame was brought to Reading by Joseph Huntley, of Huntley and Palmer fame, the philanthropist who provided a row of terraced houses for the poor. Sadly, at the official grand opening, the ones at each end were found to have developed cracks and quickly crumbled.

Probably the town's most famous temporary resident was Oscar Wilde, who, in that less enlightened Victorian time, served two years' hard labour in Reading's notorious prison for what the town's guide describes as a 'social indiscretion'. According to Lord Alfred Douglas, Oscar was as indiscreet as a nine bob note.

Reading residents of today include Uri Geller, who is something of a local campaigner. There's always something he's ringing the council to bend their ear about.

Clive Sinclair, who invented the C5, was born in Reading. Commercial success evaded his novel electric scooter as its range was limited to no more than a few hundred yards, or slightly more if you bought the optional extension lead.

Reading is proud to be the home of the Yellow Pages and what a boon they are. If you want to unblock a toilet, they'll readily find you a bulldozer to drive through the middle of Slough.

OXFORD

෨ᠿ෪

O XFORD is a fine historic city with much to offer. The name 'Oxford' came about when an observant local noticed an ox in a ford and thought it would make a nice name for a university city. It is a sobering thought that had the animal in question been a cat, our greatest seat of learning would have been situated in a suburb of Lewisham.

No introduction to Oxford would be complete without a mention of its world-famous university. So that's that done.

The first evidence of human settlement in Oxford dates from around 2000 BC with discoveries of crude arrow and spear heads. Later, a more sophisticated tribe of metal workers settled at the confluence of the Cherwell and Thames to forge their Bronze Age jewellery, which they sell on eBay.

Oxfordshire was once famous for raising fine pigs, but local bacon production began to suffer with competition from Danish imports. However, the trend reversed when it was discovered just how much water Danish bacon contained, after an Abingdon man drowned on his breakfast.

During Tudor times, the Protestant Bishops Latimer and Ridley were burnt alive in Oxford in 1555, followed by Archbishop Cranmer the following summer. After an investigation, it was discovered the General Synod Events Committee had bought a faulty barbeque.

During the Civil War, Oxford was a Royalist stronghold and it was from the city that Prince Rupert's cavalry rode north to fight Cromwell's forces at the Battle of Birmingham. The Roundheads lost and so were forced to keep it.

With the restoration of the monarchy, Oxford found favour with King Charles II, who was a frequent visitor, staying at the Old Red Lion on Merton Street where Nell Gwynn kept a room. Now Grade I listed, her bedroom has been preserved, complete with its original revolving door.

In the early 1700s, Edmund Halley came to Oxford, where he calculated that a huge comet would appear in 1987. And, sure enough, in August that year, exactly as predicted, one opened next to B&Q.

Another who worked in Oxford was Sir William Blackstone, the 18th Century jurist noted as the founding father of the United States legal system. To this day defendants can claim the Blackstone Defence, as employed by O. J. Simpson's lawyers, a device which insists every man is innocent even if he is obviously guilty as hell.

The Reverend Dr Spooner lived and lectured in Oxford. As a boating enthusiast he spent many hours renovating and maintaining local water craft. And what a reaction there was from the Women's Institute when Dr Spooner presented his lecture 'Care of Punts', ably assisted by his secretary, Mary Hinge.

William Morris, later Lord Nuffield, established car manufacture in Oxford in 1913. His first model was the famous 'Bull-Nose' Morris, so called because his name was 'Morris' and he wore a large brass ring through his nose. The Morris Organisation laid the foundations of what later became Austin-

British Leyland unveil their new model range for 1982

Morris, then BMC, then British Leyland, then Jaguar-Leyland, then Jaguar-Rover, then MG-Rover, and finally the Tsing How Kak Shanghai Trading Corporation (in receivership) Ltd. Sadly now gone, the company once provided steady employment for generations of Oxford signwriters.

There's always much excitement in Oxford when the university rowing crew defeat Cambridge in the annual Boat Race. In fact it's traditional for the eight victorious oarsmen to have their hands shaken by the mayor, while the mayor's wife bends down to kiss their little cox.

It is a tradition of Oxford colleges that they provide public baths fed by natural cool water springs for the use of weary travellers. On a hot summer's day there is nothing to beat popping into the college baths, stripping off and immediately feeling a little fresher.

Tim Henman was born nearby and as a young lad developed his tennis skills by playing alone against the side of his parents' house. One recalls his first tournament when he got all the way through to the semi-finals, only to be beaten in straight sets by a garage door.

Nearby is Blenheim Palace, seat of the Marlborough dynasty. The name derives from a decisive battle of 1704, when the first Duke of Marlborough won a great victory over Louis XIV, thus saving Europe from French domination. Blenheim Palace recently began generating its own electricity, from a dynamo connected to Marlborough's tomb.

HIGH WYCOMBE

ॐ⚛ॐ

IGH WYCOMBE is a town boasting a rich and varied past. The very name 'High Wycombe' has an interesting derivation. The Saxon word 'Wick' meant a small village community, 'Coomb' was the Celtic word for a small depression or hollow, while the Middle English 'High' has the same meaning as today. Hence the literal translation: 'Hello villagers who live in a hole'.

The town's wealth was built on the manufacture of traditional furnishings, and High Wycombe quickly became known as the 'Furniture capital of England'. Then, with the growth in demand for chests of drawers and fancy footstools, it was elevated to the tall-boy and pouffe capital of Europe.

The area first attracted pilgrims in the Dark Ages, when the sick came to take the waters at the local 'Holy Wells', which they believed could cure their blindness. This practice had to stop when, despite the warning signs, the deep wells became blocked by the many who had fallen down them.

Much of the local land formed the estate of the first Duke of Buckingham, fellow reveller and confidante of the high-living Charles II. Remnants of an old nursery rhyme mocking his antics were recently discovered in the town archive. It's difficult to make out the full wording, but it starts: 'There is an old Duke called Buckingham, whose maids say he never stops . . .'. Sadly, that's all that survives.

Close by is Wycombe Air Park. This houses a fine collection of vintage aircraft, including the Vickers Boxkite Biplane which local man Bert Hinkler flew in 1921. Racing the express train from London, he won by a full eleven minutes. At the age of 103, Mr Hinkler celebrated by repeating the event in October 2006, and beat the train by seven and half hours. It would have been more, but the chain kept falling off his bike.

The nearby Chiltern Hills are famous for the health-giving properties of their fine spring waters, but when bottles were recently discovered to contain urine, they were quickly withdrawn from supermarket shelves and moved round to the own-brand lager section.

The area is also home to many celebrities including Sporty Spice, Noel Gallagher and Kate Moss, and according to the official guide, Tim Brooke-Taylor lives within spitting distance. A facility many locals are happy to use fully.

Britain's favourite pop combo, The Goodies, whose 1976 single 'Do the Funky Jingle Bells' became that year's Christmas number 37

WATFORD

ଚ⌖ଌ

IT WAS IN THE 11th Century that the Catalonian King Wilfred came upon a site by a water crossing where he laid down the foundations of a new city, which was to become the envy of the Holy Roman Empire. With its ancient covered market, Romanesque brick towers inlaid with fine enamelled tiles, a Baroque cathedral and a former Summer Palace housing the finest collection of Renaissance artworks in Northern Europe, there are few things finer than to spend an afternoon browsing amidst its remarkable Gothic splendour; a legacy owed to that great King Wilfred of Catalonia. What a pity he never visited Watford.

Modern Watford is associated with glamour, high finance and the international jet-set, all exemplified by the town's most famous son: Nick Leeson.

Located on one of the most ancient thoroughfares out of London, Watford is the first place you come to on the way to wherever it is you're really going.

PARADISE

FOUND IT! ~~LOST.~~

BOOK I.

F Mans Firſt Diſobedience, and
the Fruit
Of that Forbidden Tree, whoſe
mortal taſt
Brought Death into the World,
and all our woe,
With loſs of *Eden*, till one greater Man
Reſtore us, and regain the bliſsful Seat,
Sing Heav'nly Muſe, that on the ſecret top
Of *Oreb*, or of *Sinai*, didſt inſpire
That Shepherd, who firſt taught the choſen Seed,
In the Beginning how the Heav'ns and Earth
Roſe out of *Chaos* : Or if *Sion* Hill
Delight thee more, and *Siloa's* Brook that flow'd
Faſt by the Oracle of God ; I thence
Invoke thy aid to my adventrous Song,
That with no middle flight intends to ſoar
A   Above

First edition of Milton's most noted work

MILTON KEYNES

MILTON KEYNES was founded in 1967, and grew steadily into a municipal borough, until in 1997 the council celebrated their 30th anniversary by applying for Unitary Authority Status. They certainly know how to have a good time in Milton Keynes.

The name 'Milton Keynes' has an interesting derivation, many believing it to be a tribute to John Milton, who wrote the trilogy comprising *Paradise Lost*, *Paradise Regained* and, in his advanced years, *Paradise I Know I Left It Somewhere*. But Milton suffered for his work, his eyesight eventually failing him completely. He would doubtless have been proud of what the town planners achieved.

With its broad avenues and boulevards laid in grid pattern, Milton Keynes is often mistaken for New York. Remarkably, there is no record of New York ever having been mistaken for Milton Keynes. However, the local townsfolk were nonetheless delighted when the French Government presented them with a huge statue of a woman holding a torch in celebration of Milton Keynes's victory in the War of Independence, and sent a bemused New York City corporation a small herd of concrete cows to mark their application for Unitary Authority Status.

In the 1980s, the city centre was further honoured on film when its railway station was used as the town hall in the Superman movies, the location chosen after the producer spotted a man in the phone box outside taking his trousers down.

Although Milton Keynes is known as a new town, anyone who believes the area has no history before 1967 couldn't be more wrong, as there is evidence of a tribe of Stone Age tool-users constructing crude dwellings in nearby Bletchley as early as 1958.

It was at Bletchley Park during World War II that the world's very first computer was installed, and its top secret output will make fascinating reading just as soon as they get the printer to work. The original buildings have been preserved as a museum with various artefacts from the period, and for a small entrance fee, visitors can be transported back to 1942. A cheaper alternative is to hop on the bus to Newport Pagnell.

Milton Keynes today has much to be proud of. It is the home of the Open University, founded in 1969 by Harold Wilson, who declared degree level education would be available to anyone with a basic passion to study men in beards and flared trousers at three o'clock in the morning. The town also boasts the huge National Bowl, probably the finest annual exhibition of sanitary-ware in Europe.

Celebrating their application for Unitary Authority Status

ENGLAND
THE MIDLANDS

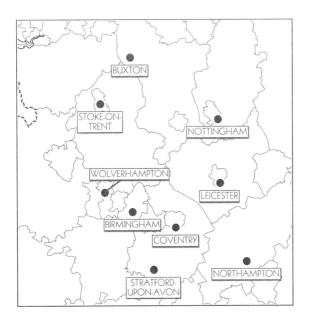

On 6 June 1963, US President John F Kennedy visited West Berlin and delivered his seminal 'Ich bin ein Berliner' speech, condemning Soviet oppression of the Eastern Bloc and their positioning of offensive missiles in Cuba, in a clear attempt to stave off the potential nuclear destruction of the planet (having previously cancelled an invitation to open the new Co-op Dairy in Northampton)

NORTHAMPTON

ℵⲤℬ

NORTHAMPTON is a town that's described as the 'Naples of the Midlands', as often as Naples is described as the 'Northampton of Lombardy'.

Originally called 'Hampton', or 'large village', the name 'Northampton' stems from the Viking occupation, when it became 'Norse Hampton'. It was in 973 AD that the Saxon King Edgar regained the town from the Norse King Gudrum, and freed its captive womenfolk, who were all highly impressed with his victory proclamation: 'I have the Hampton of a Norse'.

Northampton is ideally placed to offer much to the intrepid Midlands tourist. But a few miles away is Rugby School, where, during a football match in 1807, a player picked up the ball and ran with it, thus creating the great British sporting tradition of being sent off for dissent after a deliberate handball.

A few miles to the south of Northampton, punters flock most weekends to enjoy the Towcester Races, followed by the Food-Mixer Hurdles, and the Three Year Old Washing-Machine Handicap.

Not far from Northampton is the stately home of Earl Spencer at Althorp, which the earl insists is pronounced 'All-throp'. What a load of 'carp'. The English language itself contains many similar anomalies. There's the redundant 'G' in the word 'gnat', the unused 'K' in 'knowledge', and the silent 'P' in 'swimming baths'.

STRATFORD-UPON-AVON

∂⌘∂

TRATFORD-UPON-AVON is a fine town with a fascinating
history, mostly associated with the theatre. Thousands of
visitors flock to Stratford from all around the world to
admire the place that celebrates the career of Britain's greatest
ever theatrical name, by visiting Judi Dench's cottage.

Stratford is also associated
with a playwright called William
Shakespeare, who, it is widely
believed by scholars, may have
written several of Kenneth
Branagh's films. Little is known
about Shakespeare except that
he named one of his plays after a
brand of cigar – the classic love
story of the young blade and his
frail girlfriend: *Romeo and Slim
Panatella*.

Shakespeare's birthplace is
certain and many famous characters down the years have visited the very room in which he
came into the world, and many
have scratched their names in

*Before a groundbreaking
performance by John Gielgud as
Othello in the* Black and White
Minstrel Show, *a member of
the audience is persuaded to
buy a programme*

the glass of his window. Visitors can still make out faint signatures that include Sir Henry Irving, Mr Oscar Wilde, Miss Lilly Langtree and Mr Pilkingtons Safety Glass.

COVENTRY

৪৳৪৵

OVENTRY enjoys a fascinating history and was long known for the manufacture of fine timepieces. One J. W. Player made the most accurate wristwatch ever, but as it cost over a million pounds to make, his company went bust, exactly 36 hours, 28 minutes and 2.47533877 seconds later.

The city has several Royal connections. Mary Queen of Scots was held in Coventry and was given a small dog which she took with her to the Tower of London. The animal was there at her grisly end, even as the axe fell. Then a witness shouted 'fetch!'

The name 'Coventry' entered the language as a popular phrase during the English Civil War, when Royalist prisoners were sent to the city. As the locals were Parliamentarian, they refused to speak to them, and hence the common expression: 'Sod the Cavaliers.'

The earliest promoter of Coventry was the Earl of Mercia, who played an important role in stimulating growth for the city's founding fathers, as did his wife Godiva when she rode naked through the streets. In fact, all the townsfolk agreed to avert their gaze, except for one, 'Peeping Tom', who watched her single handed, and as a result went blind.

Another famous event in the city was a duel between Coventry's sheriff, the Earl of Hereford, who challenged the Duke of Norfolk. When the latter arrived at the city gate in search of a bride, he was called to by Hereford who asked:

'Identify yourself and your intentions toward my daughter.'
The gauntlet was cast down after the reply: 'Norfolk and Good'.

Modern Coventry is noted for its car manufacturers, including Jaguar, who, in their brief return to Grand Prix racing from 2000 to 2004, did so much to secure a remarkable five consecutive world titles for Ferrari.

Before Coventry became so involved with heavy industry, the area was famous for its finely dyed blue fabrics. With only primitive equipment, the 'woaders' as they were known, had to compress layers of cloth into vats of dye using their body weight, by sitting on the top. They are long gone, but there is a small band that continues the noble art of dying on their arse. You can often hear them on Radio 4 on Mondays at 6.30 p.m.

Coventry City's legendary goalkeeper, Dave someone-or-other, makes a superb save, much to the appreciation of City's many adoring home fans

BIRMINGHAM

ॐ⚚ॐ

BIRMINGHAM is a vibrant city which is rightly proud of its long and fascinating history. A settlement there first grew in Anglo-Saxon times and was known as: 'Beorma-ham'. 'Beorma' was a Saxon chieftain from the lowlands of Northern Friesland, and 'Ham' was what he had in his sandwiches.

After the Norman Conquest, Birmingham was recorded as a minor village in the Domesday Book of 1086, which stated that the land we know now as the city centre was valued at twenty shillings. Taking account of inflation, in today's terms, econo-mists estimate the value has risen to nearly twice that sum.

During the Middle Ages, as trade grew, many inns were established in Birmingham, which today boasts some of the oldest pubs in England. When the town was bequeathed by Henry VIII to the Earl of Northumberland, he arrived to find a Green Man, a Blue Boy, a Carpenter's Arms, and no less than three Queen's Heads. So he put them all in a bin bag and went to the pub.

The city of Birmingham is world-famous for its architectural heritage. The first parish church of St Martin's was built by William the Conqueror using architects and craftsmen brought from Normandy. That these artisans possessed specialist know-ledge unknown to the English, is commemorated in a tapestry in the chancel which reads: 'This house of our Lord was con-

structed by the grace of Norman Wisdom', just below a picture
of a little builder falling off a ladder.

The city's fine town hall was designed in 1832 by the architect
Joseph Hansom, who also designed the taxi-cabs which bore his
name. This is why the town hall mysteriously disappears without
trace when it's raining.

Birmingham's industrial origins go back to the 14th Century,
when peasants finding iron ore and coal deposits started to
experiment to produce hot smelting fires and to fashion basic
farm tools. Only after decades of failure did they realise that iron
doesn't burn and lumps of coal make lousy shovels.

But they persevered and Birmingham's reputation as an industrial centre grew steadily. By the 18th Century, the city was the
power house of the Industrial Revolution and a massive canal
system was built. With barges pulled by horses, the canals
thrived until well into the 20th Century, when they were abandoned after becoming choked with drowned horses.

With the growth of waterborne transport, Birmingham
boasted more miles of canal than Venice. Interestingly, when
Marco Polo had travelled the known world, he was commissioned by the Venetian merchant princes to establish spice and
silk routes to Cathay. Setting sail across to the shallow waters of
the Lido, he looked back across the Renaissance splendour of the
Piazza San Marco towards the Doge's Palace and observed: 'If
only Venice had more canals it would be just like Birmingham.'

Birmingham's armaments industry was greatly helped by the
English Civil War. The city supported Parliament and 15,000
swords were produced and lent to forces garrisoned to take care
of the town's womenfolk. When peace resumed, the swords

As Britain's nuclear power programme took off, enriched plutonium
was stored in many of Birmingham's public buildings

were returned, but as a symbol of what they did in Birmingham during the war, Cromwell's men continued to wear the sheaths.

Down the centuries, Birmingham armaments factories have supplied the military hardware used in every conflict from Waterloo to the Battle of Britain, and it was in light of this achievement that a special day was mooted in celebration of Britishness. The idea was to tag this on to an existing commemorative day, but no decision has yet been reached, as Trafalgar Day would offend the French, while VE Day would upset the Germans. So – too spoilt for choice then.

Modern Birmingham is the leading British producer of jewellery, making many thousands of engagement rings every year for Ulrika Jonsson.

The pioneering scientist Joseph Priestley came to Birmingham in 1788 and after three years' work discovered oxygen. This came as a great relief to the townsfolk, who had had to hold their breath up till then.

Priestley also invented the fizzy soda drink, by devising a method of forcing large quantities of carbon dioxide gas into water. He gave it to many friends, who trumpeted his achievement around the city.

Sir Arthur Conan Doyle lived and worked in Aston, where he regularly visited shops in Watson Street. It is recorded that, while short of a name for a new character, Conan Doyle spotted a sign there, and so was born 'Dr Massive Golf Sale'. Another title of Conan Doyle's was inspired by the famous printer and fellow Birmingham resident, John Baskerville. An ardent atheist, Baskerville requested that he be buried on unconsecrated ground in the garden of the family home. Sadly, he was later dug up by the dog.

The Victorian artist and poet John Ruskin married in Birmingham in 1872. However, Ruskin had led a sheltered life, and it is reported that on his wedding night he was so shocked by the sight of hair on his bride's body, that he was unable to make love until she agreed to shave her beard off.

Other famous Brummies include the political thinker

Wedding portrait, Mrs John Ruskin, Birmingham, 1872

Joseph Chamberlain, whose sons Austin and Neville also left their marks. Austin lent his name to the popular car manufactured nearby, the Chamberlain Allegro GLX, while one-time mayor Neville Chamberlain did so much to help ensure the restructuring of the city centre when he failed to prevent World War II.

Names from the arts include the poet Gerard Manley Hopkins, who became more popular when he dropped the name 'Gerard', donned a blonde wig, and sang the 1969 Eurovision entry 'Those Were The Days'. And landscapes from the brush of local Victorian artist David Cox are regularly shown by the City Gallery in the best possible setting. It's not difficult to understand why visitors flock in admiration every season when the curators announce they'll display their beautifully hung Cox collection.

The poet Gerard Manley Hopkins giving a recital

The romantic novelist Dame Barbara Cartland was born in Egbaston, but spent her working life on her country estate. The last time she visited Birmingham, on the occasion of her 80th birthday, there was an unfortunate incident when she was asked to smile for the camera and a large area of the city was destroyed in a chalk dust explosion.

The inventor Joseph Stannah worked in Birmingham on the prototype of the stairlift which bears his name. He experimented by placing his elderly mother in an electrically propelled armchair which ran on rails attached to the staircase of their home. However, much to the annoyance of his mother, when Stannah first tested his machine, it malfunctioned badly. She went through the roof.

Another famous name associated with Birmingham is the rock musician Ozzy Osbourne, who was born in nearby Aston. He is famous as former lead singer and songwriter for the heavy metal band Black Sabbath. In 1979, Osbourne left the band to embark on a highly successful solo career, and now tours the world performing to sell out audiences. So Ozzy, if you're reading this, that's who you are.

The author J. R. R. Tolkien lived in Birmingham, and it's where he wrote *The Hobbit* and *Lord of the Rings*, although some would say his greatest achievement was his work on fly fishing, written under the pen name J. R. R. Hartley.

For over 100 years, Birmingham was the home of HP Sauce, before production was moved to the Netherlands. Memories of the Centenary Celebrations in 1998 are still fresh, and particularly a celebratory address to the workers by the late Queen Mother. Her Majesty was a little frail and unable to get her words out, so they turned her upside down and smacked her on the bottom.

Advertising copy featuring Britain's first Korean restaurant

WOLVERHAMPTON

☙✤❧

THE FIRST RECORD of a settlement in Wolverhampton dates from 985 AD, when a grant of land was made to Lady Wulfruna by Ethelred the Unready, in recognition of her marrying his reluctant brother, Ethel the Unsure-about-Him.

Following Wulfruna's reorganisation of Midlands' boundaries, the only existing map of England was redrawn in Wolverhampton before being returned to the King. The process took a team of monks a total of 81 years – that was six months to redraw the map and the rest of the time trying to work out how to fold it back into its original shape.

During the Civil War, the young Prince Charles disguised himself and hid for two days in an oak tree outside the town. He was only discovered when a Roundhead soldier spotted a long-haired, 12-stone pigeon nesting above him.

The country's longest ever serving MP, Sir Charles Villiers, represented Wolverhampton. Villiers sat permanently on the Westminster back benches for 63 years until he died in 1898, from an acute attack of piles.

The Wolverhampton of today is world famous for its fine football team, known universally as 'Wolves', because they go out at night and scavenge food from dustbins.

And probably the town's most famous contemporary son is the lead singer of the pop group Slade, Noddy Holder, although

Noddy isn't his real name. His parents in fact named him: 'Hugh Pugh Barley McGrew Cuthbert Dibble Grub Holder'.

In the Middle Ages it is recorded that William Shaw, the town dog-whipper, was paid six shillings a year to expel dogs from St John's church by gripping them with wooden tongs and whipping them ferociously. He held the post for nearly 20 years, until his enthusiasm for

Wolverhampton's most favourite son: Noddy Holder

the task got the better of him when he attacked a group of golden labradors, and was subsequently banned from conducting all future tours for the blind.

John 'Iron-mad' Wilkinson built the first iron furnace in Wolverhampton in 1767. So keen was he on iron, that he built bridges, railways, houses and ships from it. The parish records reveal that, at his funeral, Wilkinson was even laid to rest in a coffin made from six-inch thick iron-plate, and that it took nearly eight weeks to cremate him.

Another famous local name is that of one Button Gwinnett, who travelled to America, later adding his signature to the Declaration of Independence. As a result, he was thrown out of the Washington Museum and put on the first plane home.

LEICESTER

❦

EICESTER is a fine city boasting a rich and varied history. A settlement is first recorded in the area during the Iron Age, when a Celtic tribe discovered ferrous ore deposits, learned how to extract iron and settled there to build their dwellings. Two centuries later the invading Romans named this tribe the 'Coritani', being the Latin word for 'people whose houses have rusted away'.

Under Roman occupation, new roads were constructed, and Leicester became the crossroads of the Midlands, with supplies of troops and goods arriving along the Via Devana, 'Via' being the Latin word for 'road' and 'Devana' meaning 'three mile tail-back'.

When the Romans left, Leicester fell under Danish occupation, and many of the city's place names emanate from its 9th Century Danish occupiers, including 'Dean Gate', 'Wyggeston Lane' and 'Unsmoked Rindless Street'.

With the Danes defeated, Christian rule returned to the city, with the Church acting as police, judge and jury. During this time, criminals were routinely rounded up by devout Christian priests, herded into the town square and summarily forgiven.

In 1485, Richard III stayed in Leicester on the eve of the Battle of Bosworth. He took lodgings at the White Boar Inn, where he famously insisted on taking his own bed. As the inn has since become a Travelodge, many guests today wisely choose to do the same.

Leicester's prosperity grew rapidly with its commerce, but 1795 saw the outbreak of the Corn Riots, when a lack of proper chiropody caused protesters to hobble painfully onto the streets.

Leicester today is very much a city of variety, with ancient architecture nestling alongside the modern. A prime example is the ornate City Hall which is based on Italianate Renaissance designs: the city's magnificent clock tower was taken from the Pallazzo Vecchio in Florence, where the city fathers are understandably keen to get it back.

The founder of the English parliament, Simon de Montfort, was born in Leicester, and one of the city's concert halls was named in his honour, after he took the title 'Third Baron de Bingo on Tuesdays'.

It was at one of de Montfort's parliaments that the five-year-old King Henry VI was knighted. During the celebration banquet, Henry was sent to bed early as punishment for not asking his mother's permission before having the Lord Chamberlain executed.

Over the following centuries, Leicester became known for the fine quality of its textile manufacture. Towards the end of the Civil War, Charles I came to Leicester and bought three items of clothing, including the two shirts he wore at his execution. Luckily, his wife had the foresight to keep the receipt for the hat.

Nearby places of interest include Melton Mowbray, home of the pork pie. The recipe for the original pie is a closely guarded secret, but is known to rely on using pork from a specific breed of pig that produces a copious amount of gelatinous fatty grease. Many breeders have successfully raised such pigs, but none has ever managed to catch hold of one.

The many well-known names associated with the town

include W. G. Grace, who, in partnership with his brother, founded the department store made famous by Mrs Slocombe and Captain Peacock.

Daniel Lambert, England's fattest man, was born in Leicester in 1770. Reaching a weight in excess of 50 stone, he became something of a local celebrity, and was eventually honoured by the city, who awarded him his own postcode.

Leicester was also the birthplace of John Merrick, whose life was immortalised in the film *The Elephant Man*, featuring John Hurt in the lead role of *Dumbo*.

This 'Spot the Ball' competition featuring a Leicester City game is from an early edition of the Daily Mail. *It was considered a little too difficult for their readership*

STOKE-ON-TRENT

֍֎֍

THIS PART of England's West Midlands is commonly known as 'The Potteries'. Famous for its manufacture of China products, buyers come to Stoke-on-Trent from the world over to obtain fine silk sarongs, chopsticks and rickshaws.

The area is also well-known for coal, iron, beer and pottery. It was in 1739 that the famous Wedgwood factory was set up at nearby Burslem. Soon their distinctive stoneware pots were in great demand by the townsfolk, who would use them to quaff copious quantities of the local ale, later taking full advantage of the fine porcelain products from the nearby Royal Doulton works.

A well-known neighbouring town which has recently become involved in the local art of brewing is Bournville. Traditionally associated with chocolate, Bournville has taken advantage of its natural springs for the production of lager, which is why there's a glass and a half of water in every pint.

But a stone's throw away is Newcastle-under-Lyme, so-named after a 'new castle' was built under 'Lyme' forest. Nearby, they constructed a feather store on the site of an old scrap yard and recycling centre. And so was born the charming village of 'Down in the Dumps'.

Famous local characters include Thomas Minton, the

inventor of 'Minton', Josiah Spode, the inventor of 'Spode', and Edward Knoblock, who luckily for some of us, didn't invent anything.

Stoke-born John Barrington Wain, a writer in the 'anti-bourgoise realist' tradition, shot to fame with his witty first novel, *Hurry On Down*. This spawned the great *Hurry On* series, including *Hurry on Doctor*, *Hurry On Nurse* and most recently, *Hurry On Ambulance, the Nearest Bed is Ninety Miles Away*.

Other famous local names include the writer Arnold Bennett, who during a visit to Paris, wrote his popular Staffordshire 'Five Towns' novels, after an exchange of ideas with Flaubert. And it's surprising what proportion of *Madame Bovary* is influenced by the industrial landscape of 19th Century Stoke. As far as scholars can make out, not a single word.

In 1925, these five surrounding towns were subsumed, and officially formed into the new city of Stoke. And what a relief it was to the long-suffering supporters of 'Burslem, Fenton, Hanley, Longton, Tunstall and Stoke-upon-Trent Rangers FC', who every Saturday had to respond to the call: 'Give us a "B"'.

According to the comedian and football historian, Barry Cryer, the great Sir Stanley Matthews comes from Stoke. Rated as the finest controllers of the ball ever, Matthews played professionally well into his fifties. (*Note: But football isn't the only place fans go to see an astonishingly old man dribbling in public. And for those who haven't caught Barry's one man show, I'm told he's 'unmissable'. So remember to take plenty of vegetables.*)

I have to thank Barry for permission to reproduce this fascinating anecdote from his autobiography *Barry Cryer, My*

Life Was a Joke, which includes several more stories about the many rich, famous and talented people that Barry has heard of.

Her Majesty the Queen does her marvellous Barry Cryer impression

BUXTON

℘ↄⅎℬ

BUXTON is a delightful spa town but has few claims to
fame. The fact that it can proudly boast that Tim Brooke-
Taylor was born there is surely proof enough. In honour
of his many achievements, Buxton recently bestowed upon Tim
the freedom of the city of Sheffield.

The town is of course world famous for high quality mineral
waters from its ancient spa. Although I am required
to point out that they are also available from other good
supermarkets. Scientists recently worked out that the
limestone-filtered water that we drink today is nearly 5000
years old, when they read on the label the words 'best before
July 4900 BC'.

An architectural highlight of the town is the Royal Hospital
which was formerly the Duke of Devonshire's Great Stables,
housing his 110 racehorses. As a result, the first four patients
contracted equine distemper. On the plus side, the hospital
garden's roses are doing very well.

Another fine local building is Chatsworth House. According
to the official guide, it contains portraits by Van Dyke and work
by Franz Hals and Rembrandt hangs in the long gallery. So best
not take small children.

Probably Buxton's most famous historical visitor was Mary
Queen of Scots, who went there to take the waters in search of

a cure for her dropsy-induced headaches. A problem that was later cured permanently by Elizabeth I.

Mary stayed at the Old Hall Hotel, where she famously scratched messages to the townsfolk on a window pane with her diamond ring. These included: 'I am the only true Queen of England' and 'why does the shower curtain never seem to work?'

No visit to Buxton would be complete without a visit to its Opera House. When permission to build was granted, the people of Buxton looked to the renowned theatrical architect Frank Matcham to design a unique construction, which he duly did, copying it from his other 27 identical unique theatres. Matcham was highly skilled in theatre design and it was his notion to have the stage sharply raked. Several years later he was called back to install a roof, and the autumn falling leaf problem was solved.

Early performances at the new Opera House included many by the great stars of the day, and it was there that the great Dame Nellie Melba was honoured by having a dessert named after her. 'Nellie Melba' was of course a stage name, she having in fact been christened 'Sherry Trifle'.

The surrounding Peak District has a rich history. It was there that the Romans fought a long campaign with the Iceni, which languished in stalemate on the River Wye for many years. However, the ferocious British tribe would always make a quick attack whenever they saw an opening in the Romans' Wye Front.

Nearby is the cavern known as the Robber Poole, named after a notorious highwayman who lived there. However, when additional troops were needed to protect the town from attack, he was pardoned after he rode non-stop to London on an unsaddled wild stallion. His reward was a small plot of land where it was reported he tended his two acres.

The nearby system of caves is well known for its underground rivers and tight-twisting tunnels, and is where potholers can come to test their skills. Alternatively, they can blindfold themselves and climb fully clothed into a chest freezer full of muddy water with a couple of paving slabs strapped to their sides.

Surrounding Buxton are the beautiful hills of the Derbyshire Peak District, where many rock climbers enjoy their sport, and, indeed, Sir Edmund Hillary came to the area to prepare before going off to Everest to become a double glazing salesman.

Like other places in the Peak District, Buxton still practises the ancient ritual of 'well-dressing'. This involves setting up a wooden sacred image covered with clay and then coating it with a mosaic of flower petals, leaves, moss and grass cuttings. The whole process can last up to three weeks and everyone is welcome. Anyone thinking they might enjoy a visit to Buxton to witness this, really ought to get a life.

NOTTINGHAM

⅋₼₰

NOTTINGHAM is a fine city with a fascinating history. The legendary people's hero Robin Hood spent his life nearby. He famously, on his deathbed, shot an arrow from his bow, asking that wherever in Sherwood Forest the arrow should land, there he should be laid to rest, and the whole area covered with an enormous plastic bubble for visitors to ride bikes and play bingo in.

It's well documented in official records that the city's original name was 'Snottingham' or 'home of Snotts', but when the Normans came, they couldn't pronounce the initial letter 'S', so decreed the town be called 'Nottingham' or the 'home of Notts'. It's easy to understand why this change was resisted so fiercely by the people of Scunthorpe.

Amongst its many attractions, the town proudly boasts 'The Trip To Jerusalem', which is the oldest pub in England, a unique distinction shared with only 117 other English pubs. Coincidentally, the

Budget restraints on the first TV series of Robin Hood *led to his Merry Men being played by cut-price actors*

oldest pub in Israel is called 'The Day Out to Center Parcs'.

Nottingham is associated with many famous names. Born in 1850, Jesse Boot founded the chain of chemists that took his name. After a few years he realised his slogan 'Buy Your Drugs from Jessies' wasn't that great, and he changed the firm's name to Boots. The business started in Goosegate Street where Jesse's father had a tiny, oak-beamed pill shop. But there was so little demand for tiny, oak-beamed pills, they decided to diversify.

The greatest bare knuckle fighter of the Victorian age was born in Nottingham, one William 'Bend-e-goes' Thompson, probably the most famous British Boxer until Frank 'Down-he-goes' Bruno.

J. M. Barrie once visited Nottingham and was inspired to write Peter Pan when he spotted an urchin in the street. What a one in a million chance that one should have escaped from the marine biology aquarium that day, thus frightening him round the corner where he bumped into a disabled pirate and a crocodile with someone's clock in its mouth. Luckily the Normans could pronounce the letter 'L' so didn't ban it.

Another famous son of the city is Albert Ball, who shot down a total of 43 German aircraft. This would have been more, but Mr Ball was eventually banned from East Midlands Airport in 1983.

Nottingham is also famous for its links with football, and Notts County is proud to be the oldest team in the English league, but they hope soon to buy some younger players. Founded in 1862, when they were the only existing club, they had to play matches against themselves for two years. One can only imagine their disappointment at finishing runners up two seasons in a row.

ENGLAND
EAST ANGLIA

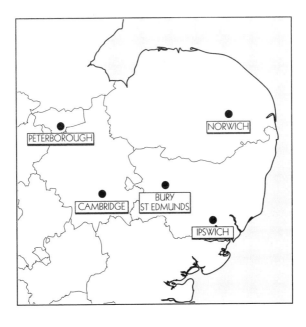

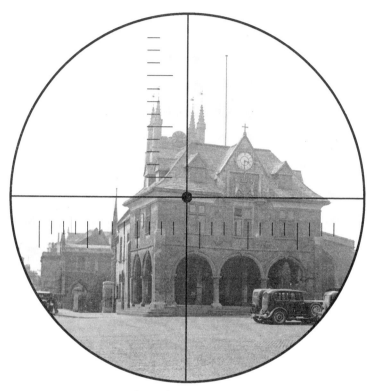

Peterborough Town Hall, 1940.
(Photo by kind permission of the German Navy)

PETERBOROUGH

ᘓᚆᘔ

ETERBOROUGH is fine cathedral city boasting a long and fascinating history. There is evidence of a Bronze Age settlement at 'Flag Fen' to the east of the city. This fenland site was discovered in 1982 when a team funded by English Heritage carried out a survey of local dykes. And when they couldn't help, the team started digging up old flood defences.

Despite the fact that they were mainly marshland, the fens were first inhabited around 35,000 years ago, the earliest settlers having walked from Europe, which was then still attached to England. Evidence exists of many from France occupying the local bogs, as they were so much nicer than the French ones.

Peterborough's cathedral has its origins in the Saxon abbey built in the 10th Century and dedicated to St Peter. As it expanded, the abbey and its surroundings were known as a 'burgh', which soon came to be called St Peter's Burgh. Eventually of course that name evolved into the one we know today: Leningrad.

Following the invasion of William the Conqueror, the Peterborough area was the last in England to submit to Norman rule. This was due to rebellions in the Fens led by the resistance fighter, Hereward the Wake, the first man in England to own an alarm clock.

It's officially recorded that Peterborough Town Hall is exactly 75 miles from London's Charing Cross. The cross was commissioned by King Edward I in memory of Eleanor, his queen. Such was the depth of his grief at the death of his beautiful bride, Edward decreed that a cross be carved ornately in marble from the Dolomites, inlaid with gold and lapis lazuli, and be erected exactly 75 miles from Peterborough Town Hall.

Catherine of Aragon came to live near Peterborough after her divorce from Henry VIII. Her settlement included estates at Kimbolton Castle, an annual pension of a thousand gold ducats, a fondue set and half a canteen of cutlery. She also got Aquitaine, but had to give it back every other weekend.

Burghley House, built by William Cecil in 1572 at Peterborough Soke, has since 1961 been home to the Burghley Horse Trials. The absolute pinnacle of equestrian eventing, spectators flock there annually from across the country in the hope of seeing a posh bird fall into a muddy pond.

Although now officially part of Cambridgeshire, Peterborough has at various times been in Rutland, Northamptonshire and Lincolnshire. One resident aged 98 who has lived in the same cottage all his life has recently been hospitalised with chronic travel sickness.

This part of England is notoriously flat and low-lying, with many areas actually below sea level. This was never a problem until the German raids of 1940, when the town hall was torpedoed by a U-Boat.

During the war, radar was invented at nearby RAF Wittering, and to celebrate the anniversary of the event, the original machinery was recently restored to re-enact its first use. At 8.30 am on the 10th October 2001, a team of technicians set the equipment running, while at the same time a restored World War

II German bomber set off from Hamburg. And, sure enough, at just after 9.15, France surrendered.

The automotive engineer Henry Royce was born in Peterborough. He formed a company with Charles Rolls, to build the finest cars in the world. It was their boast that, having turned the ignition key, you would never hear the engine running. I had an Austin Metro like that.

Just a few miles to the north of Peterborough is the town of Grantham – the birthplace of both Margaret Thatcher and Nicholas Parsons. That such a small town should produce even one great talent of world renown and adoration would be remarkable, but to produce two, well that didn't happen either.

Also born near Peterborough was Douglas Metcalfe, the pioneer of the modern home computer. Sadly, Metcalfe died in hospital in 1968, following a minor malfunction of his life support machine. His last words were: 'Have you tried switching it off and on again?'

David Beckham's Relate counsellor

CAMBRIDGE

ॐॐॐ

CAMBRIDGE is the university city that has a special place in the hearts of many, as it was there that Tim Brooke-Taylor and Graeme Garden were discovered when they were undergraduates. Luckily they slipped away in the confusion of the police raid and no charges were ever brought.

And Barry Cryer was once offered a chair there. What a nice old lady.

Other great historical Cambridge names include Sir Isaac Newton, who was Professor of Gravitational Physics at Trinity, where he also taught a little Greek, who went on to open Cambridge's premier kebab shop.

At nearby Grantchester lives the novelist, jailbird and stock market Mystic Meg, Jeffrey Archer. Archer upholds that fine tradition of English writing that can be traced in a direct line from Webster's dramatic quill, through Swift's satirical pen, right down to his own overworked photocopier.

BURY ST EDMUNDS

൭ఴ൚

THIS HISTORIC Suffolk town is swelled to overflowing during the annual carnival, when thousands of gaily-clad, olive-skinned dancers Samba through the streets to the incessant rhythmic beat of the bongo. Towards dawn, the heaving throng form into a torch-lit procession which wends its way up nearby Sugar Loaf Mountain to watch the sun rise over Copacabana Beach, their huge feathered headdresses swaying in the warm tropical breeze as they chant and sing their welcome to the new dawn. These are just a few of the rich pleasures which make this town, unmistakably, Bury St Edmunds. Or is that Rio de Janeiro?

Bury St Edmunds also became famous recently following a promotional campaign run by the Suffolk Tourist Board. There was mass rioting in the streets when, thanks to an unfortunate printing error, thousands of posters were issued encouraging one and all to 'VISIT SUFFOLK AND BURY NOEL EDMONDS'. One can only imagine their disappointment.

IPSWICH

⚔♁⚔

T HE FINE COUNTY TOWN of Ipswich is the undisputed jewel in Suffolk's crown. A beautiful county of gently rolling hills, Suffolk is bordered by Norfolk (with its historic Tudor villages and nature reserve coastline), by Cambridgeshire (with its fine university and unspoilt country-side) and by Essex.

The name 'Suffolk' is actually a corruption of 'South Folk', as the area was known until the 13th Century. It was in 1215 that King John was confronted in Ipswich by the barons before he was taken to Runnymede to sign Magna Carta. King John was of course completely illiterate: on being instructed to sign with a cross, he solemnly drew a circle. His mark was countersigned by the Bailiff of Ipswich, who inscribed the initials of 'John Reginum' alongside his area of responsibility. And thus Magna Carta was duly annotated: 'JR, South Folk'.

Magna Carta established the principle of 'Habeas Corpus' that still applies to this day – a law stating that no man in England may be imprisoned indefinitely without fair trial before judge and jury, unless of course he appears a bit foreign-looking.

Thanks to sea trade with Europe, Ipswich flourished during the Middle Ages, having close ties with the town of Antwerp, twinned with Dectwerp.

During the First World War, the pork processing plant was

requisitioned to produce ammunition. Small explosive devices similar to Mills Grenades were made there and became nicknamed 'Sausage Bombs', but without careful storage they kept going off.

In 1903 the world's first ever lawnmower was invented here, and in 1986 it was lent to the Science Museum. Ipswich still hasn't got it back.

Just along the coast is the village of Orford, famous for its ancient smoke house where herrings, salmon and eels are cured. The owner recently experimented with many different types of wood to produce a variety of smokes, with the result that the nuns at nearby Orford Convent celebrated seven new Popes in one afternoon.

By Victorian times, Ipswich was growing rapidly and horse drawn trams were introduced. However, with the construction of a power station in 1888, these old, slow conveyances were adapted to run on electricity. It was amazing how they speeded up when the horses had 240 volts put through them.

The Victorians constructed many fine buildings, including Ipswich County Hall. This houses the court where Mrs Wallis Simpson obtained her divorce prior to marrying the Duke of Windsor. However, Wallis kept her married surname, preferring not to go back to her maiden name of 'And-Gromit'.

Ipswich is a major centre for the manufacture of agricultural machinery. The town produces equipment essential to farmers' needs, such as the Revolving-Reel Combine Harvester, which separates grain from straw to ensure an efficient harvest, and the Gear-driven Half-Spinner, which turns intruders round to ensure they're not inadvertently shot in the back.

Opening in the 1920s, Ipswich Airport operated Britain's first air services to Paris. It was one of these flights that brought the great French dessert chef Escoffier to Ipswich, where he set about traditional English tarts and was soon famous for his spotted dick.

Early charity parachute jumps also took place at Ipswich airport, including the first made by a blind man. Older staff at the aerodrome remember it as a unique occasion, as they'd never before heard a golden labrador scream.

Ryanair delivers their first passenger, Ipswich Airport, 1987

In the art world, the Suffolk countryside inspired the work of Constable, Gainsborough and Lovejoy. Gainsborough is particularly associated with the area, which he toured with his easel making beautiful copies of chocolate boxes. Constable is famous for his painting in fine detail of the *Old House at Colchester*. Completed in vivid oils, the owner complained he actually only wanted his window frames re-glossed.

To the north of Suffolk is Newmarket, home of the Jockey Club. Founded in 1752, it is responsible for the control and regulation of underpants.

John Constable, made several studies for The Haywain *from this, his earliest . . .*

. . . to this, the final version.

NORWICH

༄ༀ༄

ORWICH is an ancient city that glories in a fascinating history. The first known settlers there were the Iceni Tribe, led by Boadicea in her wars against the invading Romans. Turmoil and confusion were caused by successive battles in 55, 54 and 53 BC, until someone noticed they were reading the calendar back to front.

The Iron Age Iceni were skilled in metal work, but their history is sketchy, as they were illiterate. What *is* recorded, is that 'Queen Bo Derek, bottled against the Mormon centenarians on her cheroot pulled by sick horses. Her Amy finally met deaf feet on the river Wensum, which her worriers crossed by climbing into small boots, and piddling into bottle.'

As the locality has no indigenous rock supply, Norwich was built largely of flint, and there was born the craft of flint knapping. 'Knappers' would hold a flint between their thighs to hit

Queen Boadicea at the Iceni Christmas fancy dress party, which she attended as a fireman

it with a lump hammer. These craftsmen gave us the term 'knapsack', a painful medical condition caused by missing the flint.

Later, the city became populated by Flemish weavers, who brought with them the art of canary breeding, and in a recently converted Norwich church is found the National Canary Museum, where visitors are invited to climb the tower, ring the bell and smack their heads against a small mirror.

The future King, Henry Tudor, set up base in Norwich when the houses of York and Lancaster fought the 'Wars of the Roses' for control of the chocolate sweet market.

Before entering naval college, Horatio Nelson attended the King Edward VI school. His time there is commemorated by the Norwich pub which bears his name: 'The Nelson's Arm'.

As you'd expect, Norwich City Football Club are nicknamed 'the Canaries', because of the team's long association with the popular Spanish holiday resort. This is why their supporters so regularly respond to referees' decisions with shouts of 'Balearics'.

TV cook Delia Smith lives nearby, and as director of Norwich City FC, has brought fine food to the terraces. Hence the fans' chant of: 'Who ate all the Boeuf en Croute with Cranberry Coulis?'.

Modern Norwich is famous for many products including footwear. Completion of a new shoe factory, however, has been recently delayed, due to problems with the architect. His original plan in Renaissance style Italian marble was rejected after the owners asked him for something in black in a slightly smaller size.

Some more old cobblers

Norwich is also home to the Norwich Union, the insurance company that was once claimed to be the largest in the world, although this claim was rejected, along with all the others.

Generations of the Gurney family have lived in Norwich, the Gurneys being the founding fathers of Barclays Bank. Still open for business, I popped into the original branch on my last visit, but by the time I'd got to the front of the queue, it had turned into an 'All Bar One'.

ENGLAND
THE NORTH-WEST

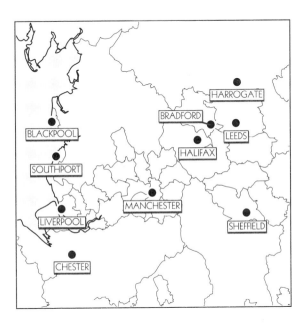

SHEFFIELD

൦൧൬

S HEFFIELD is a fine city whose history is inextricably linked with steel. The first recorded reference to steel products is found in the works of Chaucer, who mentions the famous 'Sheffield twittel', an ancestor of the modern penknife. With a super-sharp blade and immensely strong retracting spring, Chaucer describes its constant use by a pilgrim, one 'Edwin the Fingerless'.

In the reign of Elizabeth I, Sheffield was chosen to supply sets of silver plate for her household. In those days, the term 'cutlery' meant only spoons, which explains the derivation of Her Majesty's exclamation to staff, which to this day is used to begin all Royal feasts: 'Oi! Where's my fork 'n' knife?'

Prominently displayed in the city centre is the Wilkinson Memorial, dedicated to Sheffield's most famous razor manufacturer. During the city's annual Safety Blade Festival, revellers flock there to partake in the custom of decorating the statue's face, by sticking tiny pieces of tissue to it.

Behind the Memorial lies the National Museum of Shaving Requisites, where visitors can inspect a large collection of traditional shaving brushes, or stroll in the grounds, where they'll find, shivering, Europe's largest domestic herd of bald badgers.

Sheffield is a city rightly proud of its two fine football teams – Wednesday and United. Sheffield Wednesday took its name

Sheffield boasts Europe's largest public lavatory,
designed by the French architect, Jean-Claude de Pissoire

from the day on which the team played their first ever game, after taking the bus to their original ground just outside the town. If they hadn't chosen to go by First Mainline, they would have been called Sheffield Tuesday Afternoon FC.

Legendary results savoured by Sheffield football fans to this day, include Manchester United losing two-nil; Manchester United going down three-nil; and Manchester United being thrashed six-nil. None of these results had anything to do with either Sheffield team, but they are certainly great to remember.

For centuries, the city's name has been found on knives the

globe over, and in recognition of this achievement, the City Fathers erected a sign that reads: 'Welcome to Sheffield, home of the world's finest cutlery'. Not to be outdone, the nearby Peak District Council posted a sign that reads: 'Welcome to Bakewell, birthplace of the world's greatest tarts.'

Because of its metal-working industry, the area is responsible for providing many common surnames, and at one time Sheffield boasted more 'Smiths' than anywhere else in England, until the title was taken one weekend by a cheap hotel in Brighton.

Sheffield is well known for *The Full Monty*, which was filmed on location there. When the producers called for extras for the club scenes, they were amazed by the number of local women who were eager to grab the smaller parts.

Famous celebrities born in Sheffield include Michael Palin (whose name is derived from 'plannisher', someone who finished metal by hand), Sean Bean (whose family were 'banders' or craftsmen that made barrel hoops by hand) and Joe Cocker (whose family declined to comment).

MANCHESTER

꩜

MANCHESTER is a fine metropolis boasting a wealth of culture and history. According to the Office of National Statistics, Manchester is now Britain's second city. They don't say what the first one is.

As the epicentre of the Industrial Revolution, it was there that a phrase was coined that has survived to this day: 'What happens in Manchester today, happens in the rest of the world tomorrow.' So, look out rest of the world: tomorrow it's going to drizzle.

The origins of Manchester lie in a Roman settlement founded by Julius Agricola. His fortified town was called 'Mamuciam', meaning 'a hill shaped like a breast', as Agricola boasted he liked to name places after whatever he missed from home. However, he kept strangely quiet after founding the town of 'Ramsbottom'.

It was Agricola who devised modern methods of farming, and it is from him we get the word 'agriculture', and also the words 'get off moy bloody land'.

The town declined in the 5th Century, with the departure of the Romans, when raiding parties from a nearby tribe pillaged building materials from the fine houses, and to this day, marble Doric columns adorn council flats in many parts of Liverpool.

Manchester sank into obscurity for several centuries, until 1028, when King Canute decided to have one of his ten mints there, the Saxon wars having enforced the introduction of sweet rationing.

In 1485 Manchester figured heavily in the Wars of the Roses. Eventually the dynasties known as the House of Lancaster and the House of York were united by Henry VII, who combined both into the House of Fraser.

Peace reigned until the Civil War, when Royalist troops under Prince Rupert used the city as a base from which to attack near-by towns. He ordered the sacking of Bolton, when the entire town was reduced to a miserable pile of rubble. Later, funds were provided for reconstruction and work is expected to start soon.

The Royalists were soon defeated, however, and Cromwell decided to dissolve Parliament, an act made possible by the habit of constructing public buildings from sugar cubes.

The Manchester we recognise today only really appeared with the Industrial Revolution, when the city's population was housed in overcrowded slum dwellings. However, sanitary conditions were improved when pipelines were constructed to bring fresh water from the Lake District. These worked well until the 1960s, when one resident ran a bath and discovered Donald Campbell in it.

Manchester became famous for its many mills. There were woollen mills, cotton mills, silk mills, and, with the coming of Italian migrant labour, Europe's largest pepper mill, which is still in use at the Spaghetti House on Victoria Street.

Throughout the 19th Century, inventors devised many industrial machines in Manchester. There was Arkright's Cotton Frame and Hargreave's Eight-Spindle Jenny, and workers were

*Emergency plumbers improvise when five holes appear in
Manchester's water supply main*

later amazed by Crompton's Spinning Mule, possibly one of the
cruellest circus acts of the age.

In the local cotton mills, weavers were forced to pull strong
threads from the machines using their teeth. Compensation was
paid for the resultant injury which prevented them pronouncing
the letters 'F' and 'T-H'. So, they couldn't say fairer than that then.

Manchester Cathedral is rightly noted for the Gothic splendour of its architecture. Begun in the Middle Ages, construction
work continued on and off for several centuries, before being
completed, thanks to a van load of Poles arriving from Gdansk.

Manchester is proud to be home of Chetham's Library, the

oldest lending library in Britain. It was there that Karl Marx developed his arguments against the proletarian control of capital, and the rights of workers to share in the profit of labour. But the librarian said that despite all that, he was still being fined one and six. And if she caught him drawing in the margins of *Fanny Hill* again it would be half a crown.

The Manchester area has long welcomed immigrant labour from Europe. Salford was known as 'New Flanders' because of its Flemish weavers, while Ancoats became known as 'Little Italy' because it changed sides three times during World War II.

It was at nearby Trafford Park that Henry Ford's famous car factory built the massively successful Model 'T', a car he boasted you could 'have in any colour, as long it was black'. As at that time 75 per cent of the world's vehicles were Model Ts, one can imagine the frustration of trying to find yours when you got back to the car park.

The industrial labour movement was born in Manchester, eventually growing into the Trades Union Congress. So successful was the TUC that it was once honoured by having a cheese biscuit named after it. Their factory workers were served well by the collective bargaining credo of: 'one out – all out', but it failed their cricket team miserably.

The women's movement also started in Manchester, with Emiline Pankhurst and the Suffragettes, who toured with Billy J. Kramer and the Dakotas. Starting in 1910, Pankhurst campaigned noisily for women's rights outside Parliament every day from four o'clock in the afternoon. She would have got there earlier, but she always had a stack of ironing to get through first.

Another noted Mancunian was the businessman and philanthropist, Jonathan Didcott. On retiring, he sold his business there and left to tend to the poor and homeless in Liverpool, where his good work was said to be 'tireless'. Just like his car.

Manchester's first Aerodrome was opened at Trafford Park in 1911, where visitors could take pleasure trips in a novel form of aircraft powered by gas. These weren't a success, as in windy weather the pilot kept going out.

Manchester's Arndale Centre is already Britain's largest city-centre shopping mall, but there are plans afoot to add space for another 200 outlets, at least three of which aren't going to be Starbucks.

Also from Manchester was Gordon Hill, the former top division football referee. Beginning in 1958, Mr Hill officiated at over 400 matches. Sadly, he was forced to retire on medical grounds in 1972, when his eyesight suddenly came back.

A fictional name associated with Manchester is Daphne Moon, from the American sitcom *Frasier*. On the programme they frequently mention that Daphne is from Manchester, to overcome the obvious confusion caused by her accent.

Nearby Wilmslow is the upmarket suburb that's become home to many premier league footballers. However, a recent documentary following the daily lives of their wives and girlfriends had to be abandoned, when the film crew collapsed due to peroxide inhalation.

Since 2002, Manchester has been home to the Northern Imperial War Museum at Salford Quays. In celebration of their first season, the museum presented an exhibition of camouflage techniques and were proud to report that over 2000 visitors a week failed to see it.

Camouflage training in preparation for the liberation of Norway,
Catterick Army Camp, 1943

The TV antiques expert David Dickinson spent his formative years in Manchester, where as a young man he dated the girl who became his wife. He said about 1947 and worth fifty quid. Dickinson has since left the area as he says he didn't like the constant rain. It made him go streaky.

Cricketer Mike Atherton was born in Manchester. After a successful career, in 2000 he announced his retirement from first class cricket to spend more time in the England team.

Another famous Mancunian is Judy Finnigan, who presents TV shows with husband Richard Madeley. She claimed a certain notoriety when, at an award ceremony, her blouse fell open, allowing her décolletage to spill out. Ever the professional, Madeley carried on, bravely ignoring the pain of his broken toes.

Nearby Salford was the birthplace of artist L. S. Lowry. A number of his famous 'matchstick' paintings are displayed in the Lowry Centre – contents approximately forty-nine.

Nearby Wigan was the birthplace of James Thompson, inventor of the Thompson Tunneller, and a man with obvious connections to the team from *I'm Sorry I Haven't A Clue*. Designed in the 1950s, Thompson's rotary grinding machine meant tunnels all over Britain could be dug in a quarter of the time it used to take. Clearly Thompson wasn't alone in knowing how to bore the country quickly.

CHESTER

ଛ୰ଌ

C HESTER is the historic Cheshire city whose good people once returned Giles Brandreth as an MP. And who can blame them?

The name 'Chester' derives from the Latin 'Castra Devana', meaning 'a riverside garrison'. It was named by the infamous Roman Commander 'Julius Clarius' who was sent ahead of the approaching army to find a suitable location for Caesar's XXth Legion. Clarius terrified the local population when he marched into the town and proclaimed: 'I am on the look out, for Caesar's Camp.' After overindulging in the many houses of ill-repute, he became ill and spent some months being treated at the 495 clinic. Parts of a stone tablet in the city museum recount the event: 'CLARIVS CLAPPVS SIC' and go on to describe his wife as 'LIVID', which was quite an advanced age for those days.

Chester has uniquely preserved its ancient city walls. Leading up to them on the north side are the 'Wishing Steps'. Local custom says that anyone who can run up and down these 127 steps twice without drawing breath will have his wish fulfilled. This has proven to be true for several hopefuls whose wish was apparently to turn blue and collapse with oxygen starvation brought on by self-induced asphyxia.

LIVERPOOL

❧✿❧

ᴸ IVERPOOL has a linguistic derivation of some considerable historical interest. Guidebooks relate that the city took its name from two Old English words meaning 'Boggy Water', and the name is first mentioned in the Anglo Saxon Chronicle when King Edmund sailed up a creek of the Mersey and discovered 'Muddy Pools', who went on to become one of the greatest blues guitarists of the 9th Century.

However, some historians believe there is a more plausible explanation for the name Liverpool, suggesting that it may actually have come from the famous 'Liver Birds'. In fact, they reckon if Carla Lane hadn't been available to write it, the town would still be known by its old name of 'It-Ain't-Half-Hot-Mummapool'.

Famous Liverpudlians ('Scousers'), include Jimmy Tarbuck ('Tarby'), Cilla Black ('Cilla') and Les Dennis ('that bloke off the telly'). Cilla and Tarby, true to their proud roots in Everton and Toxteth, still live very close by Marbella.

Liverpool Cathedral is opened by Britain's tallest man

SOUTHPORT

ଚ୍ଚⰓⰘ

S OUTHPORT is a fine Lancashire town in the county of
Merseyside. The names of many of the small towns dotted
around Southport provide a clue to the area's Viking
past. These once included 'Alridvik', 'Tylosund Karlanda' and
'Ektorp', but were all changed when the towns discovered they
were named after a range of Ikea sofas.

Southport as a seaside resort was only really established in the
early Victorian era, when the town built Britain's first ever Pleasure
Pier. Following refurbishment in 2003, Southport won 'Pier of the
Year', much to the dismay of neighbouring Blackpool, which could
only manage second place in 'Toilet of the Month'.

Emperor Napoleon III of France lived in Southport in exile during the 1850s. When, to mark the centenary of the event, President
de Gaulle arrived on his official jet at nearby RAF Woodvale, as a
mark of respect the air traffic controllers went on strike.

Napoleon returned to Paris in 1854, and began the reconstruction of his capital, modelled on Lord Street in Southport.
Southport's town councillors returned the compliment by
providing Paris with donkey rides. The people of Paris were
delighted by this goodwill gesture, pronouncing the donkeys:
'very tasty.'

Influences of Southport's architectural style can still be seen
in Paris today. The monument at Les Invalides borrows heavily

from Southport's Norman church, while the Pompidou centre was copied from the east face of Kwik-Save.

The writer Michael Arlen was brought up in Southport. Born into a wealthy family, he led something of a playboy lifestyle, including a rumoured affair with Nancy Cunard, despite her being married at the time to the shipping magnate, James Cross-Channel-Ferry. Arlen wrote many novels and essays during the 1930s, but when his writing ability left him, he retired to raise beef cattle. Sadly he suffered from terrible butcher's block.

Southport is rightly proud to have been the home of Red Rum. The famous racehorse was trained there, running on the sands and swimming in the sea. Red Rum won the Grand National in 1973, '74 and '77 and then, in 1978, the 100 metres backstroke.

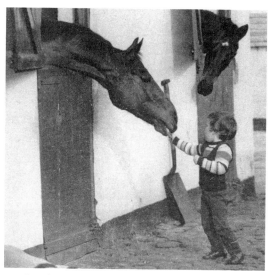

Grand National winner, Red Rum, taking a snack.
(The law was later changed, making it illegal to feed small children to horses)

Amongst Southport's many varied events, the town hosts an annual air show, with visitors enthralled by displays of air from all over the world. This year's event was won by Albert Greasby of Warrington, who gained Gold Rosettes in three categories: 'longest piece of air', 'dried air mounted on card' and 'mixed preserved airs in a sealed glass jar'. Mr Greasby puts his success down to the rich and fertile loamy soil found around his bicycle pump.

Every 12th July, Southport hosts an Orangemen's March. Last year's included Robert Kilroy-Silk and David Dickinson. Sadly, Dale Winton had to cancel as he'd contracted a nasty case of death-watch beetle.

Britain's last chief hangman, Albert Pierrepoint, lived in Southport. During a career spanning three decades, Pierrepoint is credited with executing four hundred and thirty-three men and seventeen women, including 6 US soldiers at Shepton Mallet, 200 Nazis at Nuremberg and a parking meter attendant in Wythenshawe, that last one being a private job.

Probably Southport's most famous resident is the actress Jean Alexander, who, for many years, played Hilda Ogden in *Coronation Street*. On retiring from *Coronation Street*, Miss Alexander was recruited to join the cast of *Last of the Summer Wine*, as the producers felt the show could use an injection of younger blood.

BLACKPOOL

᠙ᚠᚬ

BLACKPOOL is officially Europe's most popular coastal resort. Its first known settlement was founded by the Brigantes, an intimidating people whose warlike womenfolk terrified encroaching tribes with fearsome charges for use of hot water and the cruet set.

Little is known of the subsequent history of this area, but exciting evidence of the Emperor Vespasian's occupation was discovered recently by a local archaeologist, when a lost hoard of Roman coins fell at his feet after he got three cherries up.

After the Roman occupation, Vikings arrived in what is now Lancashire. That it was a peaceful integration is suggested by the many place names that are combinations of Scandinavian and Anglo-Saxon, including 'Layton-cum-Warbreck', 'Bispham-with-Norbreck' and 'Wigan-by-Smorgesbord-Pickled-Herring'.

These Norse settlers had arrived via the Isle of Man, where they'd gone seeking to create a new type of forward-looking liberal society. Not a mistake they'll make again in a hurry.

Blackpool became a health resort in the 18th Century, when bathing in sea water became a national craze. When it was time for the ladies to bathe, a bell was rung and any gentleman found on the shore taking a peek was fined a shilling. Court records from 1757 reveal that one offender defended himself on the grounds that he'd gone deaf, and after medical reports

Blackpool Illuminations, December 1939
(under wartime blackout regulations)

confirmed this, he was fined a further half-crown for gross public indecency.

With the growth in visitors, the North Pier was built in 1863 and its grand opening was celebrated with much drinking and revelry. Some were reported to have dived off the end despite many warnings, before coming back a few hours later to try again with the tide in.

This was followed by the Central Pier and the South Pier and, in 1902, construction of yet another was begun. Intended to stretch two miles from the promenade, by the time it reached the railway station, the builders realised they'd got the plans the wrong way round.

To compete for trade lost to the piers, the Winter Gardens decided to build a huge wheel measuring 220 feet in diameter. This spun slowly for the crowds for several years, but was never a great success and finally closed in 1926 when the hamster died.

The first of Blackpool's famous decorative illuminations were erected in Christmas 1912, when Princess Louise opened the Princess Parade. Her Royal Highness was then invited to inspect the seven miles of bulbs strung on poles, until she found the dud one that was stopping all the others from working.

In the 1930s, George Formby was a regular favourite at the Winter Gardens with his trademark gap teeth and ukulele, but stunned everyone when, in 1975, he came out of retirement in Kinshasa to fight Muhammad Ali for the World Heavyweight title.

It's in Blackpool that Jaguar cars were first built. Originally called the 'Swallow Sidecar Company', Jaguar's most successful model of the 1930s was a sports car known as the 'S. S. One Hundred'. However with the onset of war, this was thought to be inappropriate, and after much head scratching, they changed the name to the 'Two-and-Half-Litre Drop-Head Gestapo'.

Blackpool has in recent years become world-renowned as a conference centre, and is the traditional home of the TUC's Annual Conference. It was there in 1997 that they took the historic decision to scrap the old system of block votes, after one delegate ordered a hot drink and the staff delivered three point five million white coffees with three sugars.

The You and Yours *roadshow visits Blackpool*

HALIFAX

℘⌘℘

HALIFAX is a fine Yorkshire town boasting a rich and varied history. The name 'Halifax' is said to derive from a corruption of 'Holy' and 'Face', as local legend has it that the head of John the Baptist was buried in Halifax after his execution. In fact, several other Yorkshire towns are also rumoured to hold various of St John's body parts. Knaresborough is said to house his knees, while the people of Coxwold keep very quiet.

At the dawn of the Industrial Revolution, Halifax was a forward-thinking metropolis and had a police force even before London. As early as 1787 the town had constables on the beat, who, although armed with muskets, were considered both helpful and affable. But it was best not to ask one to get your cat out of a tree.

The need for new housing in Halifax during the Industrial Revolution prompted the formation of building societies. The first was suggested in 1853 by Samuel Hanson, a local businessman, who had become so disillusioned depositing his money with traditional banks, that it began to affect his marriage. As his wife relates in her diaries, Hanson would put it in, lose interest and take it out again.

A noted Halifax resident was William Herschel, the 18th Century lens-maker and astronomer. When King George III visited his observatory there, Herschel proudly proclaimed: 'With this powerful telescope, Your Majesty, I have discovered a new planet, and predict that in the future, men will travel a great distance to examine the rings around Uranus'.

Jesse Ramsden, the noted maker of theodolites was born near Halifax, and it was his pioneering work that produced the Ordnance Survey roadmaps we know today. At his funeral in 1837, mourners were surprised to see Ramsden's widow trying to read the lesson upside down.

Another scientist born in Halifax was Henry Briggs, widely considered to be one of the three greatest mathematicians of the 17th Century, the other being John Napier. Briggs excelled at university, became the father of modern mathematics and went on to encourage the use of log tables to promote his range of garden furniture.

Percy Shaw, the inventor of the cat's eye road marking, was born in Halifax in 1890. A pioneer of motoring, it's recorded that Shaw was inspired driving home one night when he spotted the reflection from the eyes of a cat walking in the road. The following night the cat was walking the other way, and Shaw invented the furry pencil sharpener.

The former High Court Judge, James Pickles, hails from Halifax. Pickles' controversial career often made headline news. He found notoriety by suggesting that young women might become pregnant between arrest and sentencing to avoid a prison sentence. Unsurprisingly, few took up his offer.

The actor Roger Moore used to live in nearby Hebden Bridge. Moore first found fame on TV as *Ivanhoe* and then as *The*

Saint, but moved into the movies where he became known as our eighth favourite James Bond.

When I'm Sorry I Haven't A Clue *visited Halifax, suppliers geared up to cater for Barry Cryer's special dietary requirements*

BRADFORD

☙⊹❧

BRADFORD is not only a tiny, picturesque village of
mellowed bath stone cottages, nestling along the banks
of the River Avon, but is also a hundred and fifty miles
away in Wiltshire. However, the Yorkshire city of Bradford boasts
a rich and varied history.

The name of the town is derived from 'Broad Ford',
because of a local river crossing which was wide and conven-
ient for dumping stolen Escorts. Originally a small Saxon
village, little of the original settlement survives apart from a
fine 15th Century cathedral, which took 194 years to complete. A construction period of nearly two centuries may seem
ridiculous to us, but of course builders were a lot quicker in
those days.

The town's prosperity grew thanks to the wool trade, and
during the Royalist siege of the Civil War, balls of wool were
even hung on the city walls to protect them from canon-fire. This
proved largely ineffective, as the Royalists hurled large numbers
of playful kittens to bat them out of the way.

The productivity of the woollen mills was raised beyond
measure in 1798 with the arrival of steam power. The engineer
James Watt, who having noticed how the steam from a boiling
kettle forced its lid open, was inspired to build his labour-saving
machine. With reciprocating three-foot piston cylinders

Eager BBC listeners are ushered to an early recording of Quote Unquote

connected by a massive cast-iron cantilever beam, Watt had created the world's first seven-ton Teasmaid.

Bradford's heritage lies in the industrial growth of the Victorian era. Thanks to the local abundance of coal and iron ore, the city boasts many educational establishments of technical excellence, producing the world's finest mechanical, electrical and civil engineering graduates, who these days go on to work in some of Cardiff's finest call centres.

Every industry at one time flourished in Bradford, and in 1952, the Bradford-manufactured Jowett Javelin motor car won the prestigious non-stop Le Mans 24-hour race, possibly the last time a British-built motor car ran for a whole day without breaking down.

Bradford was also known for the excellence of its Edwardian Theatre, which pioneered pantomime, music hall and classical drama. It was in Bradford in 1905 that the great actor-manager Sir Henry Irving, then in the twilight of his life, made his last performance. Having given a hushed audience his bloody Thomas Beckett murder scene, Irving sadly collapsed and died. It was most unfortunate, as he was actually playing Widow Twanky at the time.

Famous names associated with Bradford include the three Brontë sisters, who lived and worked there. Anne Brontë wrote *The Tenant of Wildfell Hall* under the pen name 'Acton Bell', Charlotte wrote *Jane Eyre* as 'Curer Bell', and most famous of all there was Emily, who wrote *Wuthering Heights* under the penname 'Kate Bush'.

The composer Frederick Delius was born in Bradford. He of course wrote *Sonata for Strings* and *Dance Rhapsody No. 2*, but is perhaps best remembered for *Delius – How To Cheat At Cooking*.

LEEDS

ℒⓉℬ

LEEDS is a fine Yorkshire city that boasts a rich history. At the end of the Ice Age, settlers there found the Aire Valley inhabited by woolly mammoths, an abundant source of food, clothing and ivory for tools and implements. Evidence that this species of mammoth was even worshipped has recently been unearthed in a cave inscription which reads: 'That's the wonder of woollies.'

DFS mammoth sale, 1927

By the 13th Century, Leeds had grown to become the largest wool producer in England, and the prosperity of the town was based solely on all things woollen. Consequently, the population soared from a few hundred to over 6,000, at which point loose-knit condoms fell out of favour.

In the later Middle Ages, Leeds became famous for its annual fair. Villagers would travel from the whole of Yorkshire for the event, each arriving back home with woollen garments, legs of lamb, a hog's head of mead and a dead goldfish in a plastic bag.

In 1534, one John Middleton wrote of Leeds: 'It has a praty market, and one parocky charch reasonably well buildid', for which he was awarded two out of ten in his spelling test.

During the Civil War, Charles I was a fugitive in Leeds and stayed at the Red Lion for threepence a night. Over a century later, when Lord Nelson visited, he stayed at the 'Admiral's Rest' for half a guinea, while Lady Hamilton lodged at the 'Whippet Inn' for sixpence.

1756 saw the opening of the massive Cloth Hall, which was recently restored and cleaned by a team of workers, who folded it up and took it to the laundrette.

Wool production in Leeds only began to lose prominence with the Industrial Revolution. As industry grew, the Leeds to Liverpool canal was constructed. This was opened in 1816 in great ceremony by the two cities' mayors, although it is record-ed that the Mayor of Liverpool stole the show.

Leeds was really put on the map by the Industrial Revolution and the world's first commercial steam railway opened there in 1814. Called 'The Middleton Colliery Railway', its advanced technology and efficiency of operation was considered a modern marvel, when visited by the operators of Arriva Trains Northern.

During Victorian times, Leeds became a haven for Jewish refugees from Europe, Irish workers fleeing the potato famine and Indian families from the sub-continent. Evidence of this rich cultural mix is still to be seen in the tandoori gefilter fish stalls in front of Murphy's Builders and Barmitzvah Services.

In 1872, Leeds Grammar was founded. The school still keeps a small collection of the artefacts bequeathed by their benefactor, John Harrison, who aimed to improve the city's literacy. Despite his famous philanthropy, there seems to be no trace of his stamp collection.

In 1884, Marks and Spencer opened their first shop in Leeds, and took as their trademark St Michael, the patron saint of returned cardigans.

Another famous business to start in Leeds was that of John Waddington, who opened a shop on Bridge Street, which he visited every time he threw a double six. Waddington soon built a factory to produce board games, but this was the scene of rioting by Luddites, so-named because they refused to accept the new Ludo technology.

However, Waddington's enterprise thrived until 1939, when the factory switched to helping the war effort. At one time they produced Monopoly boards for British POWs in Germany, which included hidden maps and compasses to aid escapes. One group of intrepid escapees tunnelled for eighteen months only to come up underneath a hotel, and had to pay £200 because it was on Regent Strasse.

With the advent of the First World War, the Leeds Rifles were formed and it was they who played that game of football against German troops in no-man's land on Christmas Day 1914. However, the spirit of the game was spoiled when the German centre forward executed a superb diving header and then ran off with the ball stuck on his spike.

The West Yorkshire Police crack forensics department put together a photofit picture of a notorious criminal based on extensive eye-witness statements

HARROGATE

⌒⟊⌒

THE NORTH YORKSHIRE spa town of Harrogate first became famous for the health-giving properties of its sulphur and iron-rich waters. Still operating in the Royal Bath House is its original Turkish Bath and Vichy Shower Jet Room, although the latter had to be closed during the war as the water jets kept changing sides.

In the early 19th Century, Harrogate quickly became popular with the Royal Family. And, as it was then the fashion to copy the habits of royalty, the town was soon overrun with visitors who went there to marry their cousins.

In the years leading up to the First World War, Harrogate saw many holiday visits by the Imperial Russian Royal Family, and indeed, when revolution broke out, they requested asylum there. However, a campaign led by the Daily Mail ensured they were refused, on the grounds there was no real evidence they were under any threat at home.

During the Blitz, many government offices were moved to Harrogate from London. It was amazing how far a building would travel when the Luftwaffe scored a direct hit.

There are also local connections with Admiral Lord Nelson, whose chaplain gave up the sea to become a vicar in Harrogate. Interest in the Reverend Doctor Alexander Scott was revived recently when his family sold some furniture, which historians realised had come from Nelson's flagship, when they spotted a small ad that read: 'For Sale – One Armchair'.

It's recorded that Lord Byron wrote his poem entitled 'To A Beautiful Quaker' while on a trip to Harrogate in 1806, after noticing a beautiful girl in a black robe. The poem begins:

> Sweet girl! Though only once we met,
> That meeting I shall ne'er forget;
> And though we ne'er may meet again,
> Remembrance will thy form retain.

Lost for many years, a poem in reply was recently unearthed in the Harrogate Library archive. It reads:

> Sweet Lord Byron you flatter me so
> But to your offer of love, I must say 'No'.
> For I am the vicar and aged eighty-four,
> And I think you've been at the laudanum once more.

A famous son of nearby Knaresborough was the 18th Century map-maker and road surveyor 'Blind Jack' Metcalfe, who designed the Great North Road. In no time it had stage coaches coming all the way north from London to Penzance.

Other famous names associated with this part of the world include that of Dracula. Bram Stoker, the novelist and keen sportsman, based his character on a Whitby man whom he admired as Yorkshire's opening bat.

In 1926, mystery surrounded Agatha Christie, who was discovered staying at Harrogate's Old Swan Hotel eleven days after disappearing from her home. She had become distressed after learning her husband had got a young woman pregnant, although in his defence he claimed it was the policeman who did it.

The town has a significant American population, who staff the top secret monitoring station at Menwith Hill. This has resulted in Harrogate's unusual traffic system, where the Americans drive on the right, the British drive on the left and the 4x4s drive anywhere they bloody well like.

Harrogate plays host to the world's largest annual crime writing festival. Generously sponsored by Theakstons (brewers of the strongest northern ales) this year's winning entry was an intriguing thriller, even if no one can actually remember who wrote it. They think it might have been the bloke with his underpants on his head.

This year saw Harrogate's 58th International Christmas and Toy Fair. The event was opened by the town's Mayor, but he immediately burst into tears and complained it wasn't the one he wanted.

ENGLAND
THE NORTH-EAST

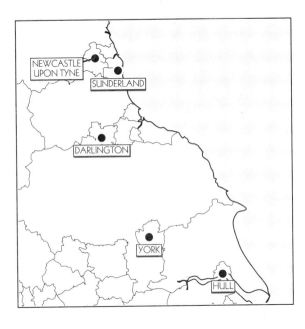

HULL

⟨ଛୃ୭ଛ⟩

KINGSTON-UPON-HULL is a fine city boasting an impressive history. The story of Hull is inextricably linked with the trawling industry, and Hull folk are often said to have fish in their blood, a condition that's baffled medical experts for years.

The original name of Kingston-upon-Hull was 'Sayercryk', an old Norse term which experts have translated as 'Kingston-upon-Hull'.

During the 7th Century, Angles and Saxons arrived in Hull, but the local Celts had them locked in holding centres, on the grounds they had blond hair, blue eyes and could speak only English.

King Edward I named the town in 1296, and shortly after, Kingston-upon-Hull received its first charter, when a party of retired newsagents from Scunthorpe was diverted on their way to Torremolinos.

During Tudor times, Hull's customs levies on Humber shipping resulted in a feud with neighbouring Beverly. Eventually, the nuns at Beverly Convent rose in revolt and laid siege to Hull. This worried Henry VIII, who sent a heavily armed force immediately he heard the town was being terrorised by the Beverly Sisters.

During the 1840s, new trawling methods meant that large

numbers of herring were landed. These were sent along to the Hull Fisheries Preserving Sheds to be smoked by fishwives, as they found them a cheaper alternative to pipe tobacco.

During the 18th Century, the British Empire expanded and it was Hull that became the headquarters of the East India Company. It was from Hull in 1746, that Clive of India set sail for Calcutta, although in those days of course, he was known as 'Clive of 26, Grimethorpe Street'.

The pioneering aviator, Amy Johnson, was born in Hull. In 1930, Amy set off on her epic solo flight to Australia with logistical support from Imperial Airways, the forerunner of BA. By the end of the first day, she'd had her lunch in Paris, her dinner in Nice and her luggage in Terminal Five. With the outbreak of war, Amy took to delivering aircraft for the RAF and often flew in Wellingtons, as their bombers were notoriously leaky.

At the start of World War II, many trawlers were converted as mine sweepers and it was Hull sailors who helped clear the way for Churchill's Allied Landings, before he expanded next door as Allied Carpets.

The mighty Humber suspension bridge was opened by the Queen in 1981. Linking Willerby with Barton-upon-Humber, the structure was at that time the longest and most expensive single-span, concrete supported bridge in the world, that connects two places no one wants to go to.

Hull's art museum houses a gallery of works by Hieronymus Bosch, where visitors can peruse his range of over-priced washing machines.

A famous name associated with Hull is that of Philip Larkin, who was a librarian at the university for thirty years. The famous poet, jazz lover and collector of pornography died there in 1985, having contracted terminal tennis elbow.

Hull is famous for its Mystery Plays and regularly stages the story of Noah's Ark. Each year there is great competition amongst Hull's womenfolk to be chosen to play the part of his wife, Joan. However, proceedings were interrupted in 1997, when real animals from the town zoo were employed. Two giant pandas, 'An An' and 'Ling Ling', who hadn't previously mated in 15 years, became over-excited and were visibly frustrated when they had to be separated by their keepers, 'Git Git' and 'Bastard Bastard'.

In the 1960s, Hull became the birthplace of the discount trading warehouse, with the Comet chain starting there. Forty years on, Comet stores pride themselves that their staff can tell you everything they know about a product in under four seconds.

Former Deputy Prime Minister John Prescott is a local MP. In buying up ex-council accommodation, his family has worked tirelessly in Hull to improve the housing standards of his family. Never forgetting his working-class roots, Prescott has himself earned considerable praise for improving the lot of Hull's many Jaguar dealerships.

Hull MP John Prescott with his bulimia counsellor

YORK

⅄ⅎℬ

YORK is an ancient and picturesque city with a rich and varied history. The first known settlement there was during the Bronze Age and was called 'Brigantia', or literally 'home of the Briganti tribe', but when Quintus Petillius and his ninth legion arrived in 71 AD, it became known as 'Eboracum', or literally, 'Not any more, it isn't'. When 300 years of occupation ended with the Roman Empire declining into a mire of drunken, orgiastic debauchery, the locals reclaimed their town and it was renamed 'Eoforwic', or literally, 'Look at the state they've left this place in'.

Very soon the town was overrun by the invading Anglo-Saxons, and reverted to Celtic rule after King Arthur's famous victory. This was shortlived, however, as Arthur fled south when a messenger arrived from Camelot with the urgent news that it was another bonus roll-over jackpot week.

By the 8th Century, York was capital of Northumbria, but during a succession of wars against the Vikings under Ivar the Boneless, the city fell several times, although not nearly as often as Ivar.

The Vikings were finally defeated in 1066 at Stamford Bridge, and with the subsequent arrival of the Normans, this pattern of history established the old centre of York much as we see it today: repeatedly overrun by foreigners.

The name 'York' has of course been adapted in many ways. There's the 'Yorkie', the staple diet of lorry drivers everywhere who like to snack on a small dog; the famous 'Yorker' was developed in York, the bowling technique that put this year's England Cricket team where they are today – opening a supermarket in Rotherham; and of course there was the Grand Old Duke of York, who famously 'had ten thousand men', the title passing down to today's Duke of York, who's ex-wife famously tried so hard to match the tradition.

York is also associated with many other notorious names from history. Dick Turpin was hanged there in 1739 after he made the journey from London in fifteen hours. And there's an interesting parallel with Turpin's exploits for anyone travelling from London today on Great North Eastern Railways: daylight robbery in the buffet car.

Guy Fawkes was born in York. In 1606, he was hanged, drawn and quartered at Tyburn, and buried at Marble Arch, Cheapside, Ludgate and Wandsworth. His co-conspirators included one Humphrey Lyttelton, who was dragged in chains to Guildford and publicly executed. Imagine the shame brought upon my family. They were OK about hanged, drawn and quartered, but *Guildford* . . .

Barratt Homes unveil their new starter home

DARLINGTON

ଧ୍ୟଡ଼୍ୟଃ

DARLINGTON is a fine town, which proudly claims to be the unofficial capital of southern County Durham. The story of Darlington's history is neatly encompassed in its coat of arms: the cross of St Cuthbert represents the town's resistance to Viking raids, a bull's head signifies the local breeding of fine cattle, and white chevrons with black lines indicate no overtaking on an urban freeway.

One of the earliest recorded events in the region was when the local King Canute, who was worshipped as God, sat in a chair on the beach and waited for the tide to come in, to prove that he was in fact merely mortal, like his subjects. His mortality was further endorsed when he was subsequently fined three shillings by the attendant for ruining a perfectly good deckchair, before walking home trailing six feet of oily seaweed and two lengths of toilet roll around his ankles.

Canute had inherited the kingdom from his Norse father, Sweyn Forkbeard, so named because of the inaccuracy of his eating habits.

Further evidence of occupation by the Vikings is provided by the names of the nearby villages of 'Selaby', 'Eppleby' and 'Killerby'. Selaby was the village where sallow grew, Eppleby the place where apples grew, and Killerby was the village where the aristocracy went bee hunting.

According to local folklore, this area was once the domain of a notorious creature called the Sockburn Worm. Such was the terror wreaked by the monster, that the Prince-Bishop of Durham himself offered a reward to anyone able to rid him of this terrible beast. The worm was eventually slain by one John Conyers, and to this very day, every year a special public ceremony is held, at which the senior member of the Conyers family has the great honour of de-worming the Bishop of Durham.

Darlington has been known by various names down the centuries, but an early version of the current name is 'Darnton', which appears in a short poem written by King James of Scotland during a visit in 1603: 'Darnton has a bonny bonny church, with a broach upon the steeple, But Darnton is a mucky mucky town, and mair sham upon the people.' Which provides exciting historical evidence that you could at that time see the top of the church from the Royal suite of the town brothel.

One of the most admired features of Darlington is St Cuthbert's Church. According to legend, the holy relics of St Cuthbert were brought to the town by monks, and concealed on the site of the current church. Some years later, the townsfolk returned St Cuthbert's relics to Lindisfarne, who were so delighted, they treated the town to an impromptu performance of 'Fog on the Tyne'.

The church of St Cuthbert was actually built in the 12th Century by Bishop Pudsey, who preached in his purple robe and wearing a spotted handkerchief knotted over one eye. His sermons often went on for over eight hours, without even the occasional unfunny joke, and would only stop when people started throwing money.

In the early 19th Century, Darlington's thriving cattle market was at the centre of an agricultural revolution. Two local farmers, Robert and Charles Colling, experimented with the breeding of shorthorn cattle, which resulted in the famous 'Durham Ox'. One prime specimen, known as the 'Comet', which weighed in at 189 stones, won many prizes at the Durham Show in 1810. Her Royal Highness Princess Louise honoured the brothers, when she personally inspected and tied rosettes on their gigantic ox.

Darlington's history since 1825 is of course synonymous with the railway, when the scheme to run a line from Darlington to Stockton was hatched by local businessman Edward Pease. He had settled in Darlington to found the local Quaker movement,

a new religion which worshipped porridge oats. Pease commissioned the engineer George Stephenson, and soon the world's first passenger railway was opened. Stephenson's engine was a wonder of single-compression cylinder technology called the 'Locomotion', which, although requiring a whole new range of skills, was remarkably simple to operate, as illustrated by this extract taken from the original instruction

Finishing touches to the world's first Teasmaid

handbook: 'My little baby sister can do it with ease. It's easier than learning your ABC's. So come on, come on, do the Locomotion with me.'

Tickets to ride on Stephenson's new engine sold briskly, and within weeks 600 passengers were catching the train to Stockton every day until, after two months, the town was completely deserted.

The Darlington of today benefits from many facilities, including its own international airport at Teesside, on the old RAF base at nearby Middleton St George. It was from there that, in 1927, one Alf Gardiner departed on his attempt to fly solo all the way to Australia. His journey went well until engine trouble forced him to ditch in Borneo, where he landed on a rubber plantation, and bounced all the way back to Singapore.

As the area of the Tees Valley around the town is well known for the proliferation of cuckoos, Darlington is home to the British Cuckoo Society, whose office is to be found on Church Street. It's actually a branch of the Halifax, but whenever they go out to lunch, they come back to find the Cuckoo Society has moved in.

SUNDERLAND

⚭✠⚭

THE CITY OF Sunderland is located in the fine county of Tyne and Wear. A settlement first appeared in the 7th Century, when Vikings stopped off on their way to Greenland. The town was therefore called 'Soenderlundt', being an old Norse word meaning 'Who was reading the bloody map?'

The Saxon King Egfrith set up court in Sunderland to rule Northumbria and fight the Vikings, who had captured Newcastle. However, after negotiations, Egfrith took the town back for a payment of twelve silver shillings. Not a great sum even then, but the Vikings couldn't afford to pay more.

Probably the most important aspect of Sunderland's early growth was shipbuilding, which began there in 1346 at the beginning of the Hundred Years War. Many vessels were built to carry troops, but recruitment was difficult, as so few soldiers were prepared to sign up for that long. Because of their long association with the making of ships, the people of Sunderland became known as 'Makems', or, more correctly now, 'Used-to-Makems'.

The family of the first US President, George Washington, came from this area. It was George Washington who led the revolt by the American colonists, as they no longer wished to be treated as the subservient lackeys of Britain. Well he certainly reversed that one. And so the War of Independence began, and soon Americans

were raining canon salvos down upon their former British allies.
A tradition they proudly preserve to this day.

The author Lewis Carroll was a regular Sunderland visitor
and set sail from there on his journey to China. Carroll's
inspiration for the name 'Wonderland' came when he heard the
word 'Sunderland', and simply substituted the first letter.
Luckily, he wasn't going to Nanking.

It was Sunderland's Chief Constable, Frederick Crawley, who
designed the first police box. His concept was taken as the model
for the Tardis, which appears large on the inside despite being quite
tiny on the outside. When Mr Crawley left the Force, he took up
photography, producing sales brochures for Barratt Homes.

Sunderland is rightly proud of its fine football team. In 1989,
Sunderland AFC were required to turn their old Roker Park home

*On its first day of opening, the new Dr Who Museum
was visited by over 120,000 (all inside)*

into an all-seater stadium, but the scheme failed when the team found it nearly impossible to play the long ball game sitting down. Instead, a site for a new stadium was found at nearby Monkwearmouth. Work on the replacement ground began in 1996, when it was labelled 'the Wembley of the North'. However,

as the city wanted it completed before the entire team died of natural causes, it was renamed 'The Stadium of Light'. That name was borrowed from Benfica's stadium in Lisbon, because of the obvious similarity between the two cities: Lisbon is a coastal city of constant sunshine, boasting Baroque and Romanesque architecture, whose cultural heritage makes it a Mecca for writers and artists, and Sunderland is also on the coast.

The Windscale works football team's most successful goalkeeper

The intrepid BBC reporter, Kate Adie, was brought up in Sunderland. Miss Adie was present at the storming of the Iranian Embassy, the invasion of Iraq, the bombing of Tripoli and three Turkish earthquakes. When she returned to Sunderland to launch a ship, the crew shot an albatross for luck.

Sunderland has recently become famous for its call centres, and is rightly known as the UK's Call Centre Centre. The city was chosen because the North East accent is rated the most trustworthy in the country. And who wouldn't believe someone who told you your call was important to them, every 10 seconds for three quarters of an hour?

NEWCASTLE-UPON-TYNE

❧⊕❧

NEWCASTLE is a fine historic city with much to interest the foreign visitor. A fortified settlement was established there in Roman times by Hadrian, the regional consul who became famous for the building of Roman Walls; in fact, by the end of his lifetime they became one of the largest ice-cream suppliers of the 3rd Century.

In the Saxon period the town was known as 'Monk Chester', because of the large number of monks there, but was subsequently occupied by marauding Vikings, when it became known as 'Danish Gitchester'.

But the city took its modern name when the old city ramparts were replaced by a 'new castle', built by Robert Curthose, the bastard son of William the Conqueror. He wasn't in fact illegitimate; that's just what customers called him when they saw his shoddy building work.

Newcastle also proudly boasts the birthplace of the electric light bulb, the gas turbine and the

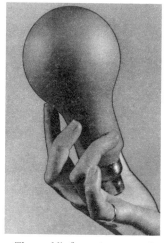

The world's first solar-powered light bulb. (Not glowing due to lack of sunlight)

steam locomotive, and it was in Newcastle that the Industrial Revolution reached its peak with the first successful demonstration of Stephenson's Rocket, following the earlier disappointment when Stephenson's Milk Bottle fell over.

As the main seaport linking England with Scandinavia, Captain Scott sailed from Newcastle to train for his polar expedition. Returning some months later in anticipation of a warm and passionate greeting from his young fiancée, one can only imagine his dismay on finding a Norwegian had got there first.

2007, Northern Rock announced 125 per cent mortgages for prime investment property

NORTHERN
IRELAND

BELFAST

☙❦❧

BELFAST boasts a rich and diverse history and the city has managed to survive troubled times with an air of optimism, recently being awarded status as 'European City of Commerce' for its services to the balaclava industry.

The name Belfast is derived from the ancient 'Bel Fierster': 'Bel' being the Gaelic for 'a river mouth' or ford, and 'Fierster' meaning 'a cheap hatchback'.

Unlike the rest of the British Isles, this area was never occupied by Romans, who arrived to find a race of backward, Stone-Age savages, when they went, by mistake, to the Isle of Man in 1982.

By the Middle Ages, the area around Belfast was noted for its manufacture of fine linen. Famous as the Handkerchief Capital of Europe, Belfast Linen Mill proudly boasted that the world wiped its nose on their products, while the Newtonards Soft Paper Mill kept very quiet. Luxury linen production continues to this day, and hankies with hand-embroidered initials are supplied to many celebrities, although Val Doonican always prefers his blank.

The National Toilet Roll Museum, Belfast

During the late 17th Century, Huguenots fled to Belfast from France, seeking freedom from religious bigotry. Not a mistake they're likely to make again.

The city and its environs can boast much of cultural and historical interest. Belfast is rightly proud of its neo-classical palazzo, where may be found a memorial to the awful *Titanic* disaster – and quite rightly, as it was possibly the world's worst ever movie.

It was from Belfast's Harland and Wolff shipyard that the *Titanic* sailed on her maiden transatlantic voyage to New York. They called at Southampton to take on passengers, Cherbourg to take on coal, and then Oslo to get the compass fixed.

The *Titanic*'s sister vessel, the *Britannic*, was converted to become a troopship, seeing action off Israel in 1946, where she was eventually sunk by a Goldberg.

1894 saw the completion of the Tudor-style Queens University, although these days they admit men of all persuasions.

During the Victorian era, many of the population emigrated to the USA, and Northern Ireland sent America no less than ten presidents, until the White House asked them to stop as they already had one.

The nearby town of Killyleagh is noted as the birthplace of Sir Hans Sloane, the founder of the British Museum, although little of interest at his family's fine mansion remains, after everything was stolen by the Egyptians.

Very much a city of tradition, Belfast is famous for its marching season, when men in dark suits and bowler hats parade in tribute to the Homepride Flour Graders.

Amongst the many famous local names is that of Eamonn Holmes. He started out in Belfast as a local reporter before going on to become very big on television.

The author C. S. Lewis was also born in Belfast. Following his success with *The Lion, the Witch and the Wardrobe*, C. S. Lewis went on to invent riot gas.

A super-economy class passenger inspects his accommodation prior to a transatlantic voyage

SCOTLAND

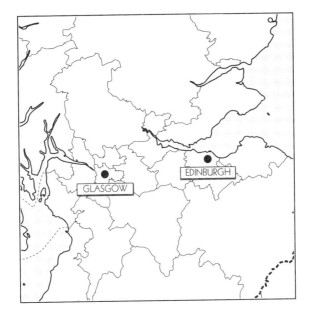

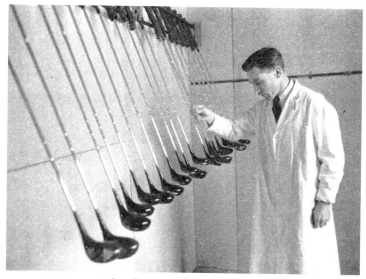

Lost Property Office, St Andrews

GLASGOW

⅋⅌⅋

LASGOW is a city that boasts many cultural and academic achievements. With an education system that is the envy of Britain, I now read that successive generations have enjoyed an amazingly high lite racy rat. Despite this, only three expressions of Scottish derivation are in regular English usage: 'Kilt', 'Haggis' and 'Partick Thistle Nil'.

Founded in the year 550 AD by St Mungo, life for Glaswegians over several centuries centred around its 'Kirk' for a people known as the 'Scottie', later joined by the 'Sulu', the 'Uhura' and the 'More Power Mr Chekovs'. It was their occasional explorations south to face the encroaching English that led to the first recorded use of the line: 'It's civilisation, but not as we know it.'

The city grew steadily and by the 18th Century was Britain's major port for trade with the New World. Sadly, rapid decline followed the American War of Independence, when the Revolutionary Colonists and their Native Indian allies fought the British to throw off the oppression of being ruled by a complete idiot called George.

Glasgow's most famous son in the field of art and design is surely Charles Rennie Mackintosh, whose family also lent their name to the popular waterproof garment. Sadly, a simple confusion over Rennie and Mackintosh, led to many braving inclement weather wearing nothing but an indigestion tablet;

although they were in better shape than those who stayed in trying to ease their dyspepsia by swallowing a raincoat. However, Rennie Mackintosh's greatest achievement must be his work in the discovery and promotion of Art Nouveau, one of the finest jazz saxophonists of his generation.

One of Glasgow's famous seagull jugglers

EDINBURGH

ଧⱭଔ

EDINBURGH, Scotland's fine capital, is very much a city of culture and elegance. Indeed Edinburgh is often called the 'Athens of the North', by many who have never visited either Athens or Edinburgh.

The city was founded by Edwin of Northumbria, and was originally known as 'Edwin Burgh', but later the 'W' was dropped. Unpopular with the townsfolk, Edwin sailed for Turkey, where they dedicated the city of Ankara to him.

Edinburgh's first charter was granted in 1329 by Robert the Bruce, who gained Scotland independence. Legend has it that Bruce drew inspiration from watching a spider, so he sat in an empty bath and refused to be flushed down the plughole until the English left.

According to the city's official records, Edinburgh became the capital in 1482, when the Scots lost Berwick. But I have startling news: I know where it is. It's just down the road on the River Tweed.

The city's political importance declined after 1707 with the Act of Union, which decreed members of the Scottish Parliament move to Westminster to run England from there.

In the early 18th Century, the Scots continued the fight for their independence, and it was during the Jacobite rebellions that Flora MacDonald became famous, when she invented margarine.

Edinburgh is the seat of the recently devolved Scottish Parliament. The Scots voted finally to split from the Union because the English notion of having a good time is to visit Edinburgh in August to watch a Hungarian juggle live lobsters in a street full of Americans while paying over the odds for a Curly Wurly deep fried in batter.

The Scottish political scene has recently witnessed a surge in support for the Scottish National Party. The SNP's cause has been greatly assisted by that famous Scottish Nationalist, the actor Sean Connery. Such is his enthusiasm for his mother country that Connery makes a principled stand in his movies and refuses to use any other accent, no matter what the role.

At the far end of the Royal Mile is Holyrood House and

On 4 March 1990, the people of Edinburgh celebrated 100 years of the Forth Bridge by painting the town red. On 5 March they started again

Queen Mary's Bath. History records it is there that Queen Mary bathed up to her waist in fine claret. One courtier who tasted the wine had difficulty describing its flavour, saying there was a hint of something he couldn't put his finger on.

Over on Princes Street is located the famous Scott Memorial. The memorial is dedicated to Sir Walter Scott of course, and not Captain Scott, although the two are easily confused, as Sir Walter also failed miserably to become the first man to reach the South Pole.

Famous names associated with Edinburgh include Sir James Young Simpson, who discovered chloroform. Making his revolutionary presentation to the Royal Surgical Academy, its members were reported to be amazed when Sir James brought in several young volunteer nurses, and proceeded to knock one out in front of them.

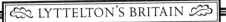
WALES

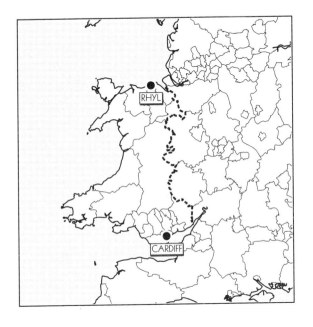

*BBC engineers prepare to receive Marconi's first broadcast
with equipment powered by sheep farts*

RHYL

ଝ⚘ଛ

RHYL, the fine North Wales coastal resort, has a long and fascinating history. According to the official history of the region, in about 1000 BC the area became inhabited by a primitive Celtic tribe who spoke a language recognisably akin to modern Welsh, this being an era before vowels had been invented.

These Celts practised ritual sacrifice in local bogs, worshipping their god 'Celdenrowd', which roughly translates as 'Call Dyno-Rod'.

Evidence of Roman occupation may be found in the bathhouse at nearby Prestatyn, where exclusively male bathers rubbed each other's bodies with olive oil before scraping it off with sea shells. This is well documented by Julius Sextus Maximus, the local camp commander.

The area then reverted to Celtic rule, and historians have recently proved that a small group led by one Owain Madog sailed from these shores for America. Their descendants were discovered in the 18th Century, as a tribe of apparently native American Indians, who were in fact obviously Welsh. As the English settlers crossed the mid-west plains, they spotted smoke signals, and realised the tribe was burning down their holiday homes.

After the Anglo-Saxons conquered England, they looked to invade Wales, but history records the Welsh defence was led by the priest who became St David. He went into battle brandishing aloft a leek to intimidate the Saxon warrior Gudrun, and when that didn't work, he twatted him with a big metal club.

During the Industrial Revolution, Rhyl became a centre of brick-making, and by the beginning of the 20th Century, many thousands of tons of bricks were going to Manchester to build housing, and to Liverpool to prop cars up.

Nearby St Asaph boasts the smallest cathedral in Britain. This is open to visitors only on Wednesdays, as that's when they take it out of the fish tank for cleaning.

The local coastline is famous for its massive castles and the first was built by Llewelyn the Great as a royal home, but this is now a sad ruin, thanks to Llewelyn the Bowen. At a ceremony in 1194, Llewelyn the Great became Prince of Wales and was required to swear allegiance to his country, marry his cousin, and have an affair with an army major's wife. In 1277, Edward I sent a massive army to conquer North Wales, and set about building a mighty castle at Harlech. Construction was overseen by 'Henri de Savoy', the French mason, who took the opportunity to sell his cut price cabbages at lodge meetings.

The Welsh coast is also noted as the last place in Britain to have been invaded by foreign troops. In 1797, a French naval force landed to be greeted by local women in their traditional scarlet costume and tall black hats. The French took them for British Redcoats and fled, clearly terrified they'd inadvertently invaded Butlins.

Inland, the area is noted for its outstanding natural beauty and down the years it has attracted many famous visitors, including Princess Margaret, who went on her honeymoon to Mount Snowdon.

At the churchyard of St Mary's, visitors can see the Victorian monument to Nicholas Hookes, a father of 41 children, along-side his wife's unusual 'Y' shaped grave.

The six miles of golden sands at Rhyl were host to the Wright Brothers, who demonstrated their new flying machine in 1907. Visitors to the town's museum will find photographs of Wilbur sat at the controls in his flying suit, and Orville sat on his lap in a duck costume.

Famous names associated with Rhyl include Carol Vorderman, whom locals remember had a Saturday job in the chemists on Flint Street. One recalls her selling him some ointment for an embarrassing itch on his consonant, vowel, consonant, consonant.

As a student in 1897, the young Albert Einstein spent the summer in Rhyl, where he began to formulate his general theory of relativity, as he worked the season as a DJ, under the stage name 'MC Squared'.

The radio pioneer Marconi made the first ever wireless broadcast from the top of the water tower in Rhyl, with the words: 'Help – I'm stuck up a water tower'.

His general theory of relativity and 'E = MC squared' was all very well, but Einstein failed to master 'i before e, except after c', twice

CARDIFF

⌘⌘⌘

CARDIFF is the proud capital city of Wales. Although officially joined with England in 1536, the principality has preserved a unique character, thanks to a resilience born of fighting successive invasions. In turn, Romans, Saxons and Vikings were repelled by tribes banding together to terrify them with their fierce displays of close-harmony singing.

The city sits on the River Taff, which gives rise to the nickname 'Taffy' for those from the Cardiff area, much in the same way as those who live alongside the River Thames in London are known as 'Homeless'.

Although the capital city of Wales only since 1955, Cardiff has many reminders of a rich history stretching back over 2000 years. To the north is the 11th Century Castle Coch, the fairytale setting for many Hollywood movies. During a break from filming there in 1959, Humphrey Bogart went to visit a local colliery, where by chance he met Ingrid Bergman and was inspired

Britain's first cinema usherette, Cardiff, 1902

to say: 'Of all the joints in all the world, you had to walk into a mine'.

But a short distance from the city centre is Cardiff Arms Park, the scene of many thrilling rugby matches. Since 1884, Wales has been a leading light in the Six Nations Cup, when the political and ethnic differences of the Irish, Scots, French, Italians and Welsh are set aside in a spirit of unity for the mutual enjoyment of sticking it up the English.

Another event to bring top class entries to Cardiff from around the globe is the annual Singer of the World Competition, possibly the greatest international sewing-machine championship of them all.

No guide to Cardiff would be complete without a mention of their fine football team. Although a fiercely proud Welsh team, Cardiff City play in the English League despite the language barrier, but they are gradually getting to grips with Italian and Portuguese.

The people of Wales have made a contribution to world events far out of proportion to the size of their population. In the 19th Century, Canada was charted by Welshman David Thompson. He spent 35 years meticulously measuring every inch of Canada and noting his findings in 77 huge volumes. He died in 1857, following a heart attack induced by the excitement of spotting some paint drying.

Thompson was also responsible for drawing the border between Canada and the USA, he being one of the few people at that time to own a two and half thousand mile, dead straight ruler.

Both of America's greatest universities – Yale and Harvard – were founded by Welshmen. Harvard is rightly proud of its graduates in law, business studies and science, and Yale its many superbly qualified key-cutters, who often also major in shoe repairs.

The notorious Chicago gangster, Al Capone, wasn't Welsh, but his right-hand man 'Machine-Gun Murray' was. Murray was the gang's 'fixer' of leading politicians and became boss for a while when Capone was in prison. Murray died in 1937, of herpes. You don't normally die of herpes, but you did if you gave it to Al Capone's wife.

The Cardiff-born singer, Shirley Bassey, generously gives up her time to support a World Wildlife Fund benefit concert

It was one Oliver Evans, an engineer from South Wales, who invented the first motorcar, in 1817. His machine weighed 26 tons, was driven by four enormous wheels, required massive amounts of fuel, and needed a ladder to get on board. The public never took to it, so he gave it to his wife to take the children to school.

The last truly Welsh Prince of Wales was Owen Glendower, who was even recognised by the English King John. In 1204, Glendower requested Joan, daughter of the King, for his wife. Mrs Glendower said she'd have preferred a toaster.

The current Prince of Wales was formally given the title at Caernarfon Castle. Amid much pageantry and splendour, when he arrived for his investiture in 1969, Prince Charles took an oath, promising as Liege Lord of Wales to 'serve, honour and protect the Welsh people from all manner of foes'. They've never seen him since.

The custom of wearing a leek to promote Welsh national pride is a long tradition. The leek is purported to possess all manner of special powers. It is not only said to be a cure for the common cold, but can also reduce the pain of childbirth. Practitioners of alternative medicine have been pushing for its use for years, but have been told they'll have to push harder.

Today, the Welsh language is the most widely spoken Celtic tongue. It is closely related to Cornish and Manx, but Cornish died out over 100 years ago, while Manx is now spoken only by one man, who continues to promote its usage. Although he recently admitted that, for all the good it does, he may as well be talking to himself.

PICTURE CREDITS